Almost

a true story

RON GARRETT

DESCRIPTIVE TEXT

Almost: A True Story is actually 52 stories that contain important life truths, gently mixed with outright lying, subtle exaggeration, and whatever else it takes to be interesting and entertaining. Think of it as a giant magazine for people who want to impress their friends by pretending they are reading an actual book. The stories are short, fairly unrelated, and typically anonymous, which is perfect for a target audience that I suspect to be riddled with Attention Deficit Disorder and who will likely to adapt these stories as their own false memories that can be shared with friends and therapists alike.

Almost a true story

My friend Ray went blind just before Christmas of 2002. It started with itchy, watery eyes and he thought he was having an allergic reaction to my dog. We suggested he take an antihistamine and he would be okay. He wasn't. So he took more antihistamine. Turns out he had very high blood pressure and the antihistamine was a bad idea. His elevated blood pressure caused the blood vessels in his eyes to burst, leaving him totally blind for life. I didn't know that your eyes could explode from anything other than walking in on your own parents having sex.

Obviously, his other friends and I felt terrible about our role in his blindness, but we took some solace in the fact that there was good news. He wasn't allergic to dogs after all! So we decided to chip in and get him a seeing eye dog. However, we had no idea at time that a service animal costs like five-THOUSAND dollars or more and sadly, we couldn't afford that.

Fortunately, we got wind of a dog that had been through all of the human assistance training but was never sold because the dog was diagnosed with Epilepsy after it's training. We got that dog for $150. Ray was thrilled that we did this for him, but he didn't know about the epilepsy because none of us were willing to admit that we bought him a faulty seeing eye dog.

Most of the time it wasn't an issue but it was hard to include him in our typical activities like dodge ball and lawn darts...because after the blindness, he sucked at both of those things on an epic level.. Eventually we got tired of his whining about being excluded so we took him with us on Spring of 2003 mountain bike trip to Colorado which, in retrospect, even non-blind people should have seen was a bad idea.

Before you go picturing a horrible image of a man and a dog strapped to a bike and falling off of a cliff, I should comfort you by stating that we had plans to ditch him long before we ever got to the actual mountain. That's what friends do. We stopped at a sporting goods store to get our permits to the mountain park before the ride. We intentionally took a really long time in the store looking at things, which obviously Ray could not do. He eventually got bored and sat down in a store display hammock and fell asleep. At this point we left him. Again, it's not like we were never coming back. We just thought we could sneak a ride in and be back before he woke up. It didn't work out that way. Mountains take a while.

Apparently Ray and his dog did have a great nap though because when the store closed no one even noticed they were still in the hammock. Everyone went home and Ray was locked inside the store, sleeping like a baby. The store closed at 9PM. We got back to the store sometime around 11PM and knew we screwed up because there were a LOT of police cars and fire trucks there.

Ray must have woken up sometime around 10 o'clock. He got up to do whatever the blind man equivalent of "looking for us" was, and his motion set off the silent alarm. Ray made it to the front door before the police showed up. Ray probably would have been fine staying calm and explaining what happened to the police. But that didn't happen. What did happen is that the police showed up at night with flashing lights, which apparently is a major trigger for seizures in epileptics...like say...maybe...Ray's defective seeing eye dog. Ray didn't even know that the cops were there yet, and didn't know his dog was epileptic so he apparently just ran, screaming, out the front door yelling "EARTHQUAKE!!!!" and dragging a spastic dog, flat on it's back, by a leash.

The cops weren't expecting that.

So they tazed Ray.

Ray wasn't expecting that.

It was a pretty surprising event for everyone actually,, but speaking purely in voltage, no one was more shocked than Ray. The police even tazed the dog, because they thought the flailing dog was rabid or something. Surprisingly, it didn't actually hurt the dog, and even went so far as to stop the seizure, which possibly saved the dogs life.

We arrived just as the ambulance guys were checking out Ray, who was still laying face down in the parking lot, but now with the addition of nice shiny handcuffs. The police were tentative as three of us approached this already weird scenario at 11PM wearing those horrible bike pants that made us look like muddy ballet dancers and wearing cleated shoes that clicked on the parking lot and furthered the oddity by making us even sound like a band of nomadic tap dancers.

The police greeted us by drawing real guns and asking us to stop moving towards them. We immediately complied because, unlike Ray, we were reacting to a visibly bad situation as opposed to just being driven impulsively by a break dancing dog in the dark.

They asked if we knew "the suspect" and we started to joke and say "that man has never seen us before" but that would not only be a lie, but it seemed like Ray was in legitimate legal trouble here. Ray used to see us. He could still identify us in a line up. We confessed to knowing Ray and knew we needed to do something to help him. We began telling the police about how Ray was a mental patient who was actually in our care but had wandered off while we were out.

Ray seemed angry when he heard this and mumbled something about "Hey guys, STOP helping me!" But you don't quit on a friend, even if they are fiercely independent. So we kept at it. Ray's mumbling was barely understandable because he appeared to have been tazed in the face, which was causing some obvious swelling, and his speech impairment was just lending credence to our story about his insanity. The fact that Ray had just come running out of a closed department store dragging a a seizing animal on a rope and yelling about Earthquakes probably didn't hurt our credibility either.

So we stood by idly, watching as the ambulance whisked Ray off to the psychiatric ward of the local hospital for a mandatory 24 hour evaluation. It wasn't the best result but it seemed better than Ray going to jail and having a permanent criminal record, and it also gave us the whole next day to get some good riding in on the mountain without having to find another way to ditch him.

I took Ray's dog back to the motel with me because the dog likes to sleep in peoples lap and I was very sore and had no idea where to rent or steal an actual vibrating recliner at this time of night. The next morning, we all discussed the possibility of trading Ray's dog out while we had this opportunity to make a switch for a more functional service animal or something more funny like maybe a Kangaroo. After a brief debate we decided to keep the same dog for Ray, not only because we still didn't have $5000 but also because after that kind of bonding, the dog was now one of us. As Ray will testify, and he probably will eventually, we aren't the kind of guys to turn our backs on a friend for more than a few hours.

I'm not sure there is really a moral of any kind to this story but if there was I think it would have to be that sometimes you have to be careful where you get your information from. You can't always trust your friends and sometimes you can't even believe your own eyes. Not everything is what it seems. Sometimes, what you thought was a unicorn, was really just a horse that had been stabbed in the face with a stick.

Something you should know

I wasn't born with any inherent interest in philosophy. The schools I went to never even mentioned the word "philosophy", much less offered a class about it. However, like most things in my life, I was led to philosophy by my pursuit of a good cheeseburger.

In high school, I dated a girl who did not share my vision for a future full of pure animal consumption. She ate weird things like lettuce, beets, and other things that I like to think killed off the dinosaurs. But alas, we did our best to make our young love work, mostly through mutual compromises composed primarily of non-eating activities like talking, playing sports, and making out. Our discord was always evident though when it came time to replenish our growing bodies with vital nutrients. She would begin to nibble on lawn clippings and I would barbeque endangered animals. It was, what some might call, a serious philosophical difference. As with most deep rifts of perspective in relationships, I fully expected her family to take her side on the issue at hand. However, this is the where the previously and eloquently foreshadowed cheeseburger comes into play...

It was a warm, but not particularly sunny, summer day and all was well with the universe. My girlfriend and I were participating in a rousing game of backyard volleyball with her neighbor's when her father emerged from his house and stepped into the philosophical hall of fame. I barely noticed him at first as he poured charcoal into an empty grill. But then the clouds parted and a ray of sun shone down upon this one lone figure in the backyard. I turned in awe as the now boring volleyball hit me in the side of my face, failing to distract me from this clear message from God. Her father casually ignored the spotlight from the heavens and slipped a cigarette into his mouth and struck a match. In one graceful swoop he swept the match past his face, instantly igniting his cigarette, before dropping the still burning match into the grill so that it too could enjoy a nice summer smoke. The flames rose like Christ from the grave, as her father quickly juxtaposed this ceremonial fire by reaching for a savory beer from the ice laden cooler at his feet. It was as if he himself was bringing all balance to the universe. Finally, as if to acknowledge the gods, her father gently laid out several pounds of animal sacrifice on this fiery alter of greatness, and then stood back in reverence with a beer in one hand and a spatula in the other. I wanted to clap, but refrained for fear that the attention I would receive for being the first to applaud would cause my girlfriend to see the tears in my eyes.

I cast a casual glance in her direction just in case I had to make up a lie about "those damn allergies" as I coyly wiped the tear from my eye. She wasn't looking at me. She was glaring at her father in complete disgust. The beer, the cigarette, and the meat were all too much for her. Her disdain was such that it brought on a heat of its own, even warmer than the noon day sun that her father was already bathing in. Feeling the death-ray, her father turned to face her. His face became overwhelmed with the loving smile that only a Father can muster. He asked his young daughter one simple question as he twirled the spatula in his non-beer hand. "How many cows you want me to grill up for ya honey?"

The obvious answer came racing back from the mouth of his young vegetarian offspring. "NONE. THAT is disgusting."

Her father feigned surprise, and took a farcical step back, clutching his beer to his chest to check his heart rate, and then finally capped off the charade with a long purposeful drag off of his unfiltered cigarette. His next words were the smoke captioned genius of my new king of introspective philosophy. "What will you do for fun...", he asked in one long exhale, "...when you are 140 years old and all of your friends are dead?".

This man was not talking about cheeseburgers. He was talking about LIFE. And I was listening. He was revealing to us, not just that cheeseburgers are awesome, but that life itself is the treat. The key to living, it seems, is to KNOW that you are dying.

The very constant condition of humanity is that it is a terminal illness. Only a fool treats a "near-death" experience as an eye opening event. Every single experience of your life is a "near death" experience. Sure, you can eat salad, but there's no guarantee of staving off the inevitable. YOU ARE GOING TO DIE. And let's be honest, more people get hit by cars while jogging than while sitting at the buffet and either one of those events is probably equally likely to induce a heart attack. Every horror movie I've ever seen has some idiot running unsuccessfully down the middle of the road from a killer. Why die tired? Sit down, have a smoke. Embrace your fate. Life is too short to get shin splints, unless you were the one doing the chasing.

There's nothing I hate worse than someone saying: "This just reminds me of how short life truly is". Really? The fact that every single one of the billions of people on this Earth that were born before 1890 is dead in a grave doesn't help remind of you of how short life truly is? The fact that there is a war, a local murder, and at least one fatal car accident on your town's news every single evening didn't drop you any clues? The fact that 1 out of every 3 people gets some form of cancer didn't seem like an indicator that life is relatively fleeting? The world is a dangerous place. Even the great television heroes "The A-Team" only made it a few seasons of miraculously skirting every potential form of death imaginable before succumbing not only to career death, but also losing Hannibal to cancer of all things! If the war against death can't be won with Mr. T at your side, what chance do YOU have in going it alone? That's right. NONE.

I don't mean to be a pessimist when I point out that you are dancing in a field of land mines. Quite the contrary. I'm just saying you don't need to be the fool who waits for their "wake-up" sign to be painted by another brush with death. The old saying "Live every day like it's your last, and someday you'll be right" is totally on point. There's a perfectly good reason why I kiss with my eyes open and shamelessly make "Nummy-nummy" sounds out loud when I'm on my fourth brownie at the endless dessert bar. I KNOW it's not truly endless.

When my girlfriend's dad stoked the charcoal fueled fires of that grill, he also stoked the fires of philosophy in the mind of this young boy. I'm happy to report that my mentor is still alive and kicking and doing just fine. Someday though, he and his health conscious daughter will both be called equally to the Great Beyond for cheeseburgers with the A-Team. Before that happens, I thought I should take this time to tell him, and the rest of things in my life: "Thanks for the burgers. I had a great time at your party."

Sea shells on a mountain

Of all the seemingly worthless advice I've ever received in my life, one of my favorite ones is "Put your best foot forward". I like it because it seems to acknowledge that I've got a second foot that is prone to not making the best decisions. That couldn't be more true. But life is a journey made up of putting both of those feet forward, one after the other, the good and the not so good, and seeing where it takes you. Having someone tell me to "put my best foot forward" doesn't seem to just imply that I should do my very best, but it also seems like a wish for good luck in starting off in the right direction on whatever my journey should be.

Today is a seemingly big day in my life. I have changed course and had to, once again, choose which foot to put forward. I have chosen to walk away from a good paying job, a place where I spend the bulk of my waking existence, and, hopefully, walk into a life where the reward is far less singular and not so easily measured. I am hoping to trade the proverbial "making a living" in exchange for the dream of "living to make it".

My job was funny in many ways. I managed a large truck stop. I never dreamed I would ever do such a thing. I never dreamed of it, because it's not the stuff that dreams are made of. I don't believe, of all the advice that a mother gives to her daughters, "When you grow up, you should marry someone who manages a truck stop" was ever something that gets said. People dream of being doctors, firemen, astronauts, and the like. No one dreams of managing a truck stop. It was not an occupation that, by title, ever filled me with pride and, hopefully, never defined me as jobs often seem to do. What did fill me with pride was that it was an honest occupation, and one that provided, financially, very nicely for myself and for my family. My job was also very unhealthy, causing me to miss every single Holiday, weekend, and most nights with my family and friends, many times working in excess of 100 hours per week. I also had exposure to many elements of life that I'd have preferred not to. Like most things, the job was both good and bad, a combination that made for a journey composed of "best" and "not so good" feet marching through a life. In most ways, I genuinely hated the job, but I was grateful for its provisions. While the job put a roof over my head and fed my children, it simultaneously bred a contempt in me so intense that it nudged me in the direction of a long overdue change. There came a time finally, when feeling like I was "putting my best foot forward" required me to step out the exit of that door.

Of all the memories I take with me from this job, the strangest, and most notable, was a chance meeting with a man whose name I don't truly recall. I think his name was Darryl. Darryl was a truck driver. He was unhealthy looking, overweight, and alone. He also seemed to be one of the happier fellows that ever walked in the door. Like many people who virtually live on the road and alone, Darryl seemed overly eager to engage in conversation. Honestly, I wasn't so excited to reciprocate. Darryl was just another face to me, nothing exciting, and certainly no astronaut. I probably wouldn't even have really listened to his unsolicited story of life, if he hadn't essentially been too proud of himself to ignore.

In the midst of our business transaction, Darryl injected the unnecessary statement, "I'm probably the only guy you'll ever meet here that climbed Mt. Everest." The only possible prompting I could imagine Darryl to have had for sharing this information was that he felt exactly the same way I did about standing in a truck stop. Darryl wanted somebody to know that he was, for lack of better way to say it, "better than this". So for one shining moment, in a truck stop in a small town, Darryl was an astronaut.

Looking at Darryl, I immediately guessed that I was about to hear a complete fabrication. He didn't look like he'd ever climbed anything other than the steps to a buffet. As sure as I was that he was lying, I played along.

"Why in the world would you ever want to climb a mountain?", I asked.

Darryl was smiling in anticipation before I ever even finished the question. Unable to contain his enthusiasm to share, he nearly interrupted me with his response.

"I asked my brother that same question.", Darryl began...

"18 years ago, my little brother told me he was leaving on a trip to climb a mountain.

I asked him, 'Why in the world would you ever climb a mountain? That seems like a good way to die."

My brother said, "We are all gonna die. I just thought it might be a good idea to be a little closer to Heaven than I am to Hell when it happens"

I said, "Brother, you're a fool. Heaven's a beach, not a mountain"

"But off he went...and he never came back. We all knew he died. We just didn't know how or where. Lots of people die on that mountain. Lots more of them than you think are still up there."

Darryl had my attention now. He proceeded to tell me how he "trained", in whatever capacity that word meant to him, and readied himself as best he could in the coming years to go and find his brother. I was still sure that Darryl was lying, but it was the most interesting thing anyone had said to me all day. Then Darryl reached in his backpack, and pulled out a box and a small photo album. The very first picture was of a mountain climber very clearly dragging a body down a snow covered mountain.

Darryl slid the picture in front of me with one hand clinging to it like it was made of pure gold, and said: "That's my brothers body."

Darryl wasn't lying. Big fat Darryl climbed the world's tallest mountain to get his dead brother's body and bring him home. Darryl was no longer a trucker. Darryl was not even now an astronaut. Darryl was suddenly THE coolest guy I ever met.

No sooner than I had put Darryl on a pedestal, his face turned sad, and his story continued.

"That's not me in that picture", Darryl said with a unwavering sadness that I can't even put into words, as he pointed to the man dragging Darryl's brother down the hill.

"Even my little brother couldn't survive that mountain", Darryl continued...

"A big old fool like me never really had much of a chance...but I made it to 14,000 feet...and then I hired a Sherpa, gave him every last penny I had, to go on up and bring my brother back."

Honestly, at this point, I was nearly moved to tears. A man's love for his brother, or anyone, on this epic level is a story will pull my heart strings every time. Darryl was pretty stoic at this point though. This pain was old and matter of fact to him now.

He quickly reverted back to his old ways of excitement though as he moved the picture aside and opened the little box.

"What you are about to see here is more rare than moon rocks", Darryl warned me, as he removed a small black rock from the box.

"This here is a sea shell....from the top of Mt. Everest. It was in my brother's hand at 22,000 feet. Even the tallest place in the world was underwater once."

This was the extent of our conversation, at three o'clock in the morning, at a truck stop in a small Indiana town, where neither one of us belonged. Tonight, for whatever reason, as I walked out the door of that place for the final time, this was the story I took with me.

I like to think that when Darryl's brother was alone on a mountain and freezing to death, and wondering "What in the Hell am I doing here?", that the last thing he saw was that little sea shell. I'll bet he smiled and thought that sea shell was thinking the exact same thing about itself. Then I think he took one last look at that massive mountain that he'd climbed, thought back to his older brother, and slipped peacefully into that goodnight, knowing that "We were both right...Heaven is a beach...and a mountain." I think that's why his brother carries that shell today. The world is not what it seems and neither is your place in it. Some of the things that people hold most precious in this world are founded in adversity and struggle. Pearls are made from the constant irritation of sand to a clam. Diamonds are forged from the intense pressure of their environment. And so, I suspect, are people. Sometimes you are the sand and sometimes you are the clam. Your role in the world is not always immediately, if ever, revealed.

The sea shell probably never knew what it meant to Darryl's brother, and there's a good chance Darryl's brother never knew what he meant to Darryl. Darryl has no idea what impact he had on me, and I don't know what effect I had on others during my year of crazy story telling in a truck stop. We were all just trying to get by as best we could, trying to climb our own massive mountains, and typically just feeling alone.

This seems like such a big day to me today, but the truth is that I know that I'll probably never know which of my steps are really going to count the most. It was just a job and most jobs aren't a life or death situation....except that it was my life and that makes it big to me. I'm just putting one foot in front of the other and hoping to get to higher ground before I die. A little closer to Heaven than to Hell, as Darryl's brother would say.

I'm not really qualified to give advice. But if I did, I'd tell my daughters: "Forget the doctor. Marry a mountain climber".

I've still got a library card

I remember standing in the bar of a VERY expensive restaurant years ago and waiting for my boss to show up to cover the ever growing bill that my customers and I were accumulating at a tremendously alarming rate. Four of us guzzled down cocktails, shots, and wine at a pace of about one every ten minutes for over an hour while we waited on my boss to join us for dinner. I finally got a return call from my boss, and it was clear to me that she was not going to be joining us. My boss, it seems, was off earning a little raise by giving her boss a "little raise" of his own. As I stood on the doorstep of a one-thousand dollar meal and a several hundred-dollar bar bill armed only with a pocketful of maxed out credit cards from college, the only words I could think to say were, "Wow, if you screw him half as hard as you just screwed me, he'll never walk again."

I shared the news with my 50 year-old multi-millionaire customers that my boss would not be joining us, and before I could finish with the fact that we should strongly consider relocating to McDonald's, they were already summoning our bartender to get us a table. I was just drunk enough at this point to let it ride while I thought of a new game plan like maybe pulling the fire alarm towards the end of the meal and running, screaming like a school girl: "We're all gonna die!" all the way back to my non-valet parked rust box six blocks away.

The bartender had been wonderful in keeping us double fisted with expensive drinks for the past 60 minutes and I suspected she was going to soon be asking me to do the small courtesy of "settling up" before we adjourned to the really, really expensive room. I had about two bucks, a 20 year-old library card, and a movie rental card on me, and I'd already given her the maxed out Visa that I only kept in my wallet because it was perfect for breaking into my apartment when I had forgotten my keys again. She used that to start a tab, because she had no clue that it was more worthless than an I.O.U. from the U.S. Government. I wasn't quite sure which one of the remaining things to hand to the sweet bartender in lieu of the $600 she would soon be requesting. "Hey baby, would you like to rent the director's cut of Star Wars on video or would you like to read it in paperback?" Knowing that I was facing a likely prospect of going to jail soon, I decided to turn on the charm.

I sauntered up to the pretty bartender, who obviously was making a career out of getting hit on by idiots like me, and tried to think of a way to insure her that I was less creepy than the other patrons because I wasn't being nice in hopes of having sex with her so much I was hoping she'd find it somehow cute that I was completely broke. Before I could even get one stupid word out of my own mouth, I heard the booming voice of my customer come from directly behind me as he too approached the bar. Clearly, he was looking at the bartender, who still had her back turned to us while washing a shot glass in the sink.

"Look at that butt!", exclaimed Jerry, "It's like a shelf. I just want to set my drink on it!". The bartender immediately turned around as Jerry continued his tirade, apparently completely unaware that he was in a fine dining establishment and holding a crystal beer mug and not holding a microphone at open mic night at the Apollo Theater. He continued speaking about the fantastic..uh...assets... of the bartender who was standing not two feet away from us and looking us in the eye. I waved my hand incredulously in front of Jerry's face and then used my other hand to jab at the thin air in front of the bartender to further provide evidence that there was no clear glass soundproof barrier between us. Jerry kept right on talking....

"Dude!", I said. "Your force field is down! Abort! Abort!"

Jerry never had a clue what I was talking about and, with each passing word, was driving me closer and closer to jail.

I finally did what any self respecting businessman would do in this scenario. I picked up a $50 tip from the table behind me and slid it over to the bartender. "Please excuse my friend", I said, while already walking away, "..and transfer that bill to the table please. I'll get you another fifty on the way back..." She raised a finger to stop me and muttered something but I was already off to the next room, pretending not to hear her.

We took a seat at the table of impending doom and opened the menus that, of course, provided no pricing at all. As the old saying goes "If you have to ask, you can't afford it." I had to ask. But I didn't. Because at this point, it didn't matter. For all intents and purposes, it was me who was down the road at the hotel with my bosses' boss, getting my head slammed into the headboard time and time again. "You guys wanna start with an appetizer?", I said. 'In fact, let's a get a few. They all sound good." Even death row inmates are entitled to one last good meal.

I spent the next hour devouring some of the most deliciously overpriced food I'd ever eaten, while listening to Jerry drunkenly describe what he'd like to do to every woman within earshot of our table. I didn't care anymore. "Waiter, keep the drinks coming...."

I was surprised to see that dinner bill came in just a hair under $800 for the four us. Add the $600 bar bill and obligatory $280 tip and I was only looking at about $1680 for the dinner. It might as well have been a million dollars. At this point, my only concern was keeping the final bill from hitting that table as I had yet to locate the fire alarm.

The waiter came by, smugly clenching the little leather folder that housed the bill I'd never pay. "Would anyone care for dessert?"

"AWWW, HELL YES!", Jerry exclaimed, rocking his chair back on two legs and rubbing his belly like the millionaire heathen hillbilly I'd come to know in the last two hours. "These belly's don't grow themselves!". With that, Jerry just smiled and added..."Hey, you got a wine list? I need something to wash all this down with."

The waiter looked, happily, in my direction for approval. Sure, why not? What's another $1000 that I don't have? "Bring it on", I said.

The wine list DID have pricing. And that's actually a bad thing. When you have to alert people who normally don't ask what things cost as to what THESE things cost, that means it's expensive. There were bottles of wine in excess of ten-thousand dollars. I'm guessing it must have been bottles full of the blood of dead Popes. I can't imagine crushed grapes costing more than my car. But they did.

Mercifully, after some half-hearted menu scanning, Jerry decided that it was not a wine night after all. "You like cognac Garrett?". I truly didn't know the answer to that. "I don't believe I've ever had it Jerry." At this point Jerry informed me that tonight was "my lucky night". Really Jerry? Cause it doesn't feel lucky....

Jerry proceeded to order some form of cognac in a language that was clearly not my own. And I was okay with that until the waiter in the very expensive restaurant did the single scariest thing that a waiter in a very expensive restaurant can do. After hearing Jerry's order, the waiter said just one word.

"Seriously?"

The clearly excited waiter was not asking a rhetorical question. He wanted to know if we were seriously ordering whatever it was he thought we were ordering. I knew that was NOT a good sign. I too looked at Jerry and said "SERIOUSLY?". Even though I had no idea at all what was going on. I just knew it wasn't good.

The waiter once again looked to me for approval and once again I made the executive decision.

"Bring it."

Moments later, the waiter returned with a cart but instead of handing us the mystery drinks, he laid a beautiful leather bound register on the table and asked us each to sign the document. "Thank God", I thought to myself, "Maybe this is the financing application I've been waiting for." But it wasn't. It was a just a register of the very exclusive people who had taken part of whatever this very exclusive drink was. Jerry scratched his name on the bottom line and slid the book over to me, where I wrote something along the lines of "Jesus forgive me" and closed the book before handing it back to my super excited server.

The waiter then handed each of us a giant crystal snifter that contained a surprisingly slight amount of beverage. Jerry hoisted his glass like a proud Viking and nearly shouted the pleasant toast "What's in this glass will thrill your ass!" and then he swirled the drink once, took a big sniff of it, and slammed it back like a shot of whiskey. Having no sense of smell of my own, I wanted to ask Jerry: "When you huffed that drink just now, did it smell like fear to you too?" But I didn't. I just raised my glass to the hillbilly king and slammed it back with shaking hands, spilling at least half of it on my face in the process.

'You like that Garrett???", exclaimed Jerry. "You want another?" Without even waiting for my answer, Jerry used his evil finger to gesture to the waiter that another round would be in order. The waiter no longer looked to me for approval.

I slowly began sipping the next glass of Satan's own nectar as Jerry blurted out "Hey buddy, you got a cigar list?"

I spit out my drink in way that would make any whale's blow-hole blush. The air in front of me became full of glistening mist and I swear that I saw a rainbow briefly appear in that blast of what was very likely a $1000 spit-take. It was almost pretty. Almost.

Clearly now concerned with my most recent response, the waiter once again looked to me for approval.

Overwhelmed with the spirit of Jerry, I nearly replied with his now famous war cry, "AWWW, HELL YES!" Because, really, at this point....why not? Hey, while you're at it, bring it out on that bartenders ass will ya? But of course, I didn't say anything at all. I just shrugged. I think this was also about the time that I began to cry inside.

"Yes sir, a cigar list would be great."

This was most certainly the last stop before prison and I still hadn't found that stupid fire alarm. My boss wasn't coming. Well, she probably was, but certainly not in a way that would help me. There was no one that I could call at ten o'clock on a Friday night and ask "Hey buddy, would you mind driving downtown and discretely paying a $5000 dinner charge for me?" I wondered, perhaps aloud, how much money the clinic would give the restaurant in exchange for draining all of the plasma out of my body until I was dead. I heard they pay good money for plasma....

The cigars arrived quickly, and I let Jerry choose one for me. I knew nothing about cigars but I thought it would be nice to start smoking while Jerry regaled us with the story of whatever it was that we were drinking and about how it had been recovered from an 1800's shipwreck and we were drinking perhaps one of the last barrels in the world. Nice. The thick cloud of smoke, whirling around him, helped complete the image that Jerry might actually be SATAN.

About this time, I backed up my chair and leaned over to tie my shoes. This is an important thing to do before you run out on a four-figure dinner bill. While I was already in the doubled over position, it was hard not to go ahead and throw up from raw fear. On the table above me, I heard the echoing boom of the final bill being dropped on the table like thunder from the sky. It occurred to me then that all I really needed to do was fall forward from my chair to complete the true look of the fetal position I was now in. "Mommy...", I whimpered. "Mommy, I'm scared..."

Then in an amazing twist of redemption, Jerry, A.K.A. SATAN, yells out from across the table. "Garrett, why don't you let me get this one? You can come up and take me out next time."

Even over the symphony of trumpets and angels singing in my ear, I actually heard a sigh come from my own butthole as it released from the tightest clinch in mankind's history.

"Oh no Jerry", I said as I slid the bill immediately over to his side of the table. "You sure?"

Jerry paid the final bill but I had already paid quite a price myself. As I left the restaurant to go find my boss and stab her in the face repeatedly with a really beautiful butter knife I had stolen from the restaurant, I mentioned to Jerry, on the way out "Don't forget to tip that bartender bro. Remember you promised her $50 earlier."

"Oh, did I?, asked a puzzled but gullibly drunken Jerry.

"Yep", I said as I ran out the door to taste the sweet non-prison air. Just outside the door I realized that I had forgotten my credit card at the bar. I patted my pockets instinctively and had that sudden and bad feeling that I had forgotten something else. My apartment key was nowhere to be found. My "spare key" Visa card was back inside the scariest place I'd ever been. I just left it there. I didn't need it. I had just had the first hand proof that "every time God closes a door, he opens a window." I knew I'd be fine.

I'm going to offend EVERYBODY

I was sitting in an office meeting when I was in my 20's. I don't remember what led up to it but I know that I made a joking comment, out loud, about my deep seeded desire to kill lots of people. I also recall my boss immediately asking to speak to me in private. We adjourned to another room where my boss informed that not one, but two of the five people sitting in on that meeting had had family members murdered by serial killers. Seriously. What are the odds? Well, with me...usually about 100%.

Although I felt like a jerk, I'm angry that I have to feel like a jerk. Jokes about serial killing are SUPPOSED to be funny. Why? Because Serial killing is not supposed to ACTUALLY exist.

I'm going to say racist things. Then I'm going to follow up my racism with sexism. Then I'm going to sprinkle some inappropriate religious jokes on top of that conversation, and serve it all up publicly with a nice healthy side order of something else that will surely offend entire groups of people that I didn't even know existed. Why would I do this? The answer is obvious. I'm a racist, sexist, blasphemous, and evil person...with an admitted penchant for serial killing.

OR...there is another, entirely unfathomable possibility at work here. That second, unimaginable option, is that all of this stuff is SUPPOSED to be funny. How can that be? Maybe because it's not SUPPOSED to happen. These aren't supposed to be categories of hate and suffering, they are supposed to be categories of humor. They are supposed to entertain you based on their complete shock value, not horrify you because of your true life flashbacks. Because I'm not a serial killer, I think I'm entitled to be angry that those are being taken away from me.

Don't get me wrong, I have my strong dislikes, like rap music, superfluous shirt buttons, and I have people I don't care to associate with, but I feel like they've earned my scorn on individual merits. I can't truly love everybody, and not just because I can't afford to buy that many Christmas presents. I genuinely think some people suck, but I would never truly make fun of someone, or bully anyone, because I think that's mean, and I like to think of myself as merely insensitive instead of outright cruel. But if you are my friend and you get a finger cut off in an accident, I'm going to give you one day to adjust, I'm going to be sincerely sorry for you, and then I'm going to send you a coupon I found for 10% off Gloves, with a note attached that says "Oh, did they mean 10% off the price?". Yeah, I'm a jerk, but if you're truly my friend, I'd hope you'd do the same for me.

My best friend is Asian Indian, but not really. He's from the same hillbilly Midwestern U.S. town as me. But he's had to deal with people waving flags in his face after 9/11 because he looks Middle Eastern. Is that complete crap? You betcha. Do I still make fun of him? You betcha. He's my friend. It's my job.

Guess what else? I've got gay friends. There are huge debates about how "tolerant" we are supposed to be about that topic, particularly by my fellow Christians that get caught up in the "morality" of their "sexuality". How funny is that? Morality and sexuality in the same sentence? That's a hoot. I'm not here to judge, I'm here to talk with a lisp and make homosexual jokes to homophobic guys and make them uncomfortable. Not because I care, but because it's fun.

I was seeking a special favor at an upscale restaurant with a large group of friends when I wrongly addressed our waiter, the only representative of his establishment, as the "ambassador of his people". Of course he was a black man, and everyone immediately assumed that I was making a racist statement as opposed to a silly comment about this man being the face of the restaurant. I'm sure the waiter assumed that too. There were collective gasps and looks of disgust thrown in my direction and I should have felt bad. But I didn't. Because my "racist" remark was only construed as racist by those thinking racist things. Maybe I should get a prize for being the only person at the table to not have considered that our server was black. The only thing I cared about is that he was bringing me food, and I'm glad that the Civil Rights Act allowed him to do that....you know...before he and I were either one even born. I'll bring him food when he comes to my job. And then we can go to a comedy club and laugh at some black comedian making fun of the way white people dance...like we are supposed to. I'm sure, like my Indian friend, that this guy experiences actual racism from intentional morons and I do feel bad, because that isn't SUPPOSED to happen. Because, again, it's not a category of hate, it's a category of comedy. Men and women, black and white, dogs and cats, Christian and Muslim, whatever... singling out any one of those groups and failing to make fun of them is discrimination, and I simply won't stand for it.

I'll defend your right to be you and you'll defend my right to be me, and if either one of us infringes on those rights we'll go to war and kill each other. It's the way of the world. It's not SUPPOSED to happen, but it does. In the meantime, I maintain my right to make fun of you, regardless of age, sexual orientation, religion, or whatever and if you are going to be my friend, you'd better do the same for me. No need to be mean, just funny. If you can't live with that, I'm going to kill you all. Seriously. Unless that offends you, in which case I'm truly sorry. Yes, I'm sorry. Sorry that you are a nine-fingered gay black Indian Jew and that you suck at hockey. But call me, we'll do lunch...cause I've got some blonde jokes I'm dying to share with you.

17

Seventeen years ago on this day, I was sitting in a truck stop in western Ohio. I wasn't on my way to anywhere. I was already there. The truck stop was the end of the line. It was Thanksgiving Day, and I had just broken up with a girlfriend, my brother was out of town, my parents were in Florida, and I had just moved to a new city. It was an odd Thanksgiving to be sure, but the sheer oddity did nothing to curb my hunger. The only thing open was a truck stop, and while that may sound like the desperate last resort of a desperate man, the truth is that I knew in advance that this particular truck stop had THREE different kinds of gravy on their buffet. I may be lonely and pathetic at times, but I'm no idiot when it comes to knowing who does or doesn't have the illusive BACON gravy in their Holiday line-up.

Emotionally, I was fully prepared to sit at a table in a world I didn't belong to, and saturate my bloodstream with endless bowls of bacon gravy, grilled sausage gravy, and hot sausage gravy until my heart rate slowed to such a pace that I was no longer able to muster up the blood flow to hoist another fork load to my face. And then I would nap. Clearly, it was God's plan for me and I'm not one to argue with the Lord on a Holiday.

The truck stop buffet had two visible cooks and one waitress, but she was there in body only. I didn't blame her. She seemed sad and lonely too but she was also being paid, and probably DID have somewhere else she could have been. There were only two other patrons in the entire establishment, a man, and a woman, and both were sitting at tables by themselves. I mumbled something about the joys of bacon gravy while walking back to my table and that somehow started a conversation with the man.

As I feared, it was only seconds later that he picked up his plate and sat down at my table, "asking" if he could join me, as he was already arranging his utensils within the confines of my personal space. I wasn't here to make friends. I was here to make cholesterol. But I didn't have the heart to tell the guy "no". It was only moments more before he whistled across the room and shouted for the lone remaining patron, whom he seemed to already know as "Honey", summoning her to join us.

Thus began my first Thanksgiving with a random homeless hitch-hiker and a lonely hooker. I don't refer to this as my "first" such occasion because of it becoming an annual occurrence, since I wasn't going to make reservations for the next year with them, but I'm not dead yet so the potential for an encore remains.

I actually had a very interesting lunch that day, and the conversation was very candid about pretty much any subject that came up. No one was trying to impress anyone. We all had already been exposed as unworthy so there was no point in faking something better at that point. A part of me wondered how truly a man is measured by the company he keeps. And upon further reflection, I prayed that there was no truth to that at all.

The fact that I saw us as random homeless dude, a lonely hooker, and then myself as something....well...more, revealed to me that I was probably the worst person at the table. I really don't think that the either of them were judging me at all. We were supposed to be three people eating dinner at a table. Nothing more.

There was no prize here for being "better" than anyone else. If there was ever truly a circumstance were no posturing was required, this was surely it. No one was going to win a free slice of pie for being the coolest one at the table. Suddenly, I was THAT guy. The guy that I hate. The guy that is driving his piece of crap in the fast lane on the freeway and when you go to pass him, he speeds up for no reason, like he has to win some imaginary race. Yeah, I was THAT jackass. I certainly wasn't the boy that my mother raised, eating with someone else's son and someone else's daughter. I was just THAT GUY that I'd become.

It was probably that shame that got me wondering if I should buy the meals for all of us. But I wouldn't have sincerely been buying meals for them, I would have been just unsuccessfully bribing my conscience. I wanted to feel better about...uh...feeling better. What better way to do that than by flaunting my money to the have-nots?

Honestly, I'm making this out to be a bigger deal than it was. I wasn't writhing in torment and inner struggle here at the table. I was still plowing through gravy bowls like an out of control bus through mud puddles, and genuinely enjoying some wild and freaky conversation with some very deep and intense humor that was born of horrific suffering. This whole "deeper meaning" of my feelings was just a side note. Because tomorrow I wouldn't care. Thanksgiving would be over and the gravy all gone. I'd forget about this whole affair, other than to joke that I ate lunch at a truck stop with a hooker and a homeless dude. Yet somehow, this was the meal that, seventeen years later, defines the Holiday season for me.

I joked the other day about how much I hate when people say they got a tattoo as a reminder of something in their lives and how people should also consider A.D.D. medication or scrap booking if they truly need a reminder of something that happened in their own life. It's it a big deal, you'll remember it. Do I need Thanksgiving to remind me to be grateful that every single day of my life is a bounty at my discretion? Do I need the grotesque commercialization of Christmas to buy a big screen television to remind me of a God? Am I going to participate in charity because I'm helping or because I'm helping me to feel good about the times that I won't help later? Does it matter?

Truthfully, I don't expect to find the answers to those questions in this lifetime. And 363 days out of the year I probably won't be looking for those answers. But once again, seventeen years later, I spent the first seventeen hours of today in a truck stop. I was talking to a customer named Perry at 1:26PM today when he reached out to me and told me that he thought he was having a heart attack. Turns out, Perry was right. I called 911 and sat at the restaurant table with Perry until the paramedics arrived. Perry asked me, if I would mind praying with him for a minute, just in case this was "it" for him. And I wondered, would he be praying if he wasn't afraid that he might die in moments? Does the reason even matter?

Thanksgiving is just a day. It's just one time a year that you scoot your junky car over to the right lane and stop trying to beat other people in a contest that doesn't even exist. It's just one day a year to focus on something you knew you were supposed to be doing all along. But one day is a pretty good start. I guess what I'm saying is, maybe that tattoo wasn't such a bad idea after all.

And now... a word from our sponsors

Like most spouses, my wife and I frequently discuss the prospect of murdering one another. I remember broaching the subject gently, in the early days of our marriage, when we used to cuddle up on the couch and watch whatever was on the television. On this particular occasion, the show was Dateline NBC. The fine folks at NBC planted millions of evil seeds in the heads of viewers by offering up the casual knowledge that the average cost of hiring someone to kill for you was a paltry 2500 US Dollars. I had always imagined such a big job to cost more but, apparently, murder unions (a.k.a. street gangs) have become so intensely competitive, that the consumers can enjoy rock bottom rates on homicide in most major cities.

Upon hearing this news, I gazed coyly over at my "life partner" to reevaluate our whole "till death do us part" thing. I could see that similar wheels were already spinning in her head. I briefly considered, as I'm sure she was, the enormous costs and hassle of a nasty, bitter divorce, before quietly stating, "Geez, total dissolution for less than the cost of your next engagement ring....that sure seems like the more practical way to go...". She nodded gently in agreement while spitting out the wine that I had just poured for her.

One of the many advantages of murder in lieu of divorce is that sometimes you also get the benefit of a cash reward, in the form of insurance money. That's a far cry better than PAYING an attorney for your matrimonial emancipation. It's not often that I quote the great prophet, Charlie Sheen, but he once eloquently stated: "I don't pay hookers for sex. I pay hookers to go away when it's over." Imagine his joy if the hooker not only went away but also left him a winning lottery ticket and maybe a nice ham sandwich on her way out the door. That's what life insurance is.

That all seems like a great fantasy, but it seems like these days murder is getting so hard to get away with. I blame all these darned CSI shows for making everyone aware of "real evidence". Don't get me wrong, I still haven't seen any of the old bleach companies go out of business but I can't help but think that just saying you spilled red Kool-Aid on the rug will make as many rich widows as it used too. No, murder has changed. Like everything else, the new world order is driving the old "Mom and Pop shops" of murder right out of business. These days, you NEED to go corporate.

Sure, "accidental ingestion" of rat poison might still get the job done, but it's a onetime payout. You get a little life insurance, or a life-time vacation to a penitentiary, but then that's it. On the other hand, if you get REALLY lucky, and your spouse happens to "trip" into the oncoming path of a federally owned mail truck, you could be looking at what the kids like to call "Double dipping". That's life insurance, AND a tasty lawsuit.

Ever wonder why no one filed a lawsuit against Vlad the Impaler or sought a cash settlement from the Bubonic Plague? Well, two reasons really....first: pretty much everyone actually died, making it hard to sue. Second: Vlad and the Bubonic Plague neither one had access to federal funding (I.E. the ability to actually PRINT money).

I'm not sure exactly when or how it happened, but somewhere along the line, CASH MONEY became the actual currency not only for hiring a killer but also for compensating the survivors of those who were killed. It kind of makes you wonder why no one has thought to streamline the process and actually just pay the families of people they want to kill to actually do the killing, thus eliminating the need for a "middleman" assassin. For whatever reason, it just doesn't work that way.

I understand the need to pay a person to kill for you. Stabbing someone in the face 1000 times with a fork can be hard work, sometimes even requiring the stabber to have to buy a new shirt. There certainly SHOULD be monetary compensation for both of those things. However, I'm not totally clear on, for example, why if I choose to smoke cigarettes for 20 years of smoke inhalating goodness, my children can sue a tobacco company for my "wrongful death" after I take my last wheezing breath? If "wrongful death" carries a financial penalty, then shouldn't we clearly define "rightful death" and perhaps even offer a cash prize to the perpetrator? Shouldn't killing an annoying street mime carry the same cash value of my being killed in a nasty work related accident? I mean a LIFE is a LIFE right? That brings me back to my original statement. The difference is corporate sponsorship.

I think the word is starting to spread. If the shopping mall collapses today, an attorney will probably beat an ambulance to the scene. Life is a terminal condition. We are all going to die. But if we can assign BLAME for our deaths to someone with real money, that certainly will help the survivors to heal. Plus, financial restitution is punishment to someone for their murderous negligence. They should feel the impact of what they have done. And what is the most sensitive organ in the human body? That's right, the pocketbook. We're practically marsupials when you look at it that way. Another reason to sue for death money is that a family has lost a provider. The tragic brake failure that your boss might endure on the already dangerous mountain drive home might create "opportunities" at the office, but it sure makes it hard for his family to keep their country club membership when his checks stop rolling in. Worse yet, they might actually have to stop doing smaller things, like eating...or sleeping indoors. I get that. That's worth money.

Marriage is actually what started this whole thing about life having cash value. Insurance has been around for a long time, but it used to be called a dowry. A dowry is described by the New World Encyclopedia as:

a gift given by the bride's family to the groom and the newly formed household at the time of their marriage.[1] Historically most societies have had brides go to their husband's families, and often women could not legally own property. The husband would be primarily responsible for the economic prosperity of the household, while women would care for children and the household needs. When a woman or girl married into a family that was agricultural, she often was welcomed as another worker. In families that were more prestigious, however, she may have been viewed as another mouth to feed, and the dowry was an important sign of her gratitude for becoming a member of her husband's family. The earliest dowries were usually land entitlements, but later were attached to sentimental and decorative items as well as various commodities and even later to CASH money.

The point here is clear....corporations have once again displaced the "Mom and Pops" of the worlds. When families stopped paying dudes to marry chicks, we had to come up with corporate based "insurance" as a system of compensating people for killing each other. It would have been nice to get that money up front, when we could BOTH enjoy it...but these days, it looks like just one of us is going to be growing old with a new Porsche.

A 40 for my homeys

I met a fairly odd fellow today at the gas station. He had a parrot on his shoulder and that's simply something you don't see often in public these days. He also paid for his bill in gold one-dollar coins. I think that was no coincidence. This fellow fancied himself to be a pirate. Because this man, who was so clearly a pirate in the eyes of a 40-year-old me, it made me think of the Jimmy Buffet song: "A pirate looks at 40". The Buffett song served primarily to provide a soundtrack for the moment in my head, but also reminded me that it was indeed after noon and time for my daily margarita.

I think if there is ever a time for deep reflection and intensive life planning, it's during the consumption of Margaritas. So it naturally occurred to me to invite this pirate for a drink. This move, I think, was construed as a homosexual advance, and immediately dismissed by the clearly homophobic land pirate. I guess he thought I presumed him to be the OTHER kind of pirate. I didn't. I just thought that a pirate probably had some keen insights that would be nice to hear over a tasty beverage. But instead of learning what that might be, I now have an old dude who walks around with a bird on his head thinking that I'M THE WEIRD ONE? Whatever.

Forget that guy. I'll get my own parrot. No...actually....that's a bad idea. Not just because I don't want to increase my chances of having my shoulders pooped on in this life, but also because of that danged old birthday I'm having. See, Parrots live to be up to 75 years old. I'm 40. What kind of responsible pirate buys a bird without the intention of having it be a "life partner"? I mean, geez, the only people who do that are coal miners... and even they just use a Canary, which is probably not long for this world anyway. I don't know why the Canary doesn't enjoy the extended lifespan of the Parrot, but I presume it's because they don't know how to unwind the way Parrots do. I think if the Canary ever spent a few years aboard a nice Pirate ship in the Caribbean, it would probably add some time to its life. A good vacation does that you know.

The bird issue is just a microcosm of the bigger picture here. My being too old to buy a Parrot means that I'm also, technically, too old to be a pirate. THAT SUCKS. I grew up believing the lie that you can be anything you want to be when you grow up. What they don't tell you is that you have to START EARLY...and also that there can be only one Mr. T.. Apparently you are supposed to be constantly working towards a goal in order to actually achieve it. Thankfully, that only applies to lofty goals. I typically wake up with much lower expectations like "Hmmmmm....bacon sounds really nice today. I wonder if I can score some...?". Then when I do, which is usually quite easy, I feel fantastic about myself and what I've accomplished with the day. It usually takes very little planning and the rewards far exceed the effort. AND AND AND AND...you are NEVER too old to buy bacon.

But if I woke up with dreams of grandeur, like "Being a pirate sounds great today...I wonder if I can do that?". Stealing a boat, making a lifetime commitment to a Parrot, and plundering others typically requires FAR more effort than scoring a few pieces of bacon.

Do I really want to be a Pirate? Not necessarily. It just irritates me that I no longer qualify for some of the criteria involved in having that option. That's what age does to you, but I'm okay with getting old. In fact, I've always been more than a little creeped out by the common expression "being comfortable in your own skin" because it seems to imply that there is a fairly horrific alternative, like: "Hey Dave, I'll be honest, I'm just not really comfortable in my own skin... and I can't help but notice that you and I are about the same height... Hey...um....do you lotion?".

However, I'll also admit that the other phrase "Age is just a state of mind" was probably made famous by someone without Osteoporosis or Congestive Heart Failure. Getting old is tough, but more for living than fear of dying. It's always a little harder when someone totals your brand new car as opposed to the one you've already gotten the mileage out of. Time is tricky like that. Days keep sneaking in on the coat tails of the ones before it like the way our parents used to sneak their buddies into the drive-in movie theater in the trunks of their cars. 40 came in like a ninja on the heels of 30. It's like a giant birthday conga line to the grave.

I was just thinking that if I died today, I'd be really content... although I'd wish that I'd have used up the last of my sick days at work this week and bought a few more things on "one-year/same as cash" terms about 11 months ago. Overall, I'm really happy and have been virtually every day of my ever lengthening life. Forty is a pretty good age to accept the fact that I won't be a movie star or that I probably won't ever really go back to school. I'm probably not ever going to win the lottery and, apparently, I'm not even going to be a pirate. The Mr. T thing is obviously TOTALLY out of the question now.

So where does that leave me at 40? Is it time to give back to the world? Is it time to start worrying about leaving a legacy and struggling for immortality? Am I finally old enough to stop excusing myself, or pretend like I didn't even notice the farts that sneak out when I'm walking around the BINGO parlor on Wednesday nights? 40 definitely seems like it should be a crossroads of some sort. But I don't see any signs. The hairs still go gray just one at at time.

Certainly my impending demise inches closer but I still don't feel the need to stay up all night tonight carving my face on a mountain. It would be pretty sad if old age was really the only thing that motivated me to knock out a "bucket list", and even sadder yet if I would have waited until now to make such a list. I may or may not have a long time to go but I feel like I'm already in the "bonus". Anything from here on out is pretty much gravy...and I LOVE me some gravy.

I guess the summary is...what is 40 like? Just like 39. Which was just like 38...or was it 27? Damn Ninjas.

I don't need a Parrot anyway. I've already got a boat and a bottle of rum...and apparently a little more time. I think I'll go ahead and dream big for a little while longer. But just to be on the safe side, I'm still probably gonna have some bacon in the morning. Sometimes, a lot of small victories are just as good as one big one.

The gentle art of baby tossing

I was in my swimming pool yesterday, seeing how high I could throw my one year old baby, when my eight-year-old asked me if I thought this was maybe a bad idea. I assured it her that it was the work of pure genius and that I had a long and storied history of baby tossing. She asked what would happen if I "forgot to catch her". While I appreciate the attentiveness of my eldest child and that she has noted my intense level of A.D.D., I promised her that even I would never "forget" to catch a baby that I had personally just launched into the air. The only reason I wouldn't catch a thrown baby is because I had done it so remarkably well that the baby actually achieved orbit, and I would still likely catch her when she re-entered the atmosphere on the following calendar day....although I might let her fall slightly into the pool first just to cool her off. I hear that re-entering Earth's atmosphere can make an already toasty summer day even more uncomfortably hot.

There are a three good reasons that baby tossing SHOULD BE done:

1. It's incredibly fun. Not just for the tosser, as even the tossee also will generally squeal with delight... Nothing beats a hearty belly laugh from a baby, especially as it fades off into the distance and then comes rushing back towards you.

2. It teaches a child trust...without the more permanent conse-quences of the old method of Russian Roulette, which was really dumb luck more than it was trust anyway. (I'm not angry Dad. I know you had a bad shoulder so guns were just easier than throw-ing a fat kid like me)

3. Well, obviously there aren't THREE good reasons to throw a baby but it is so much fun that we can count that reason twice.

Between years of baby tossing, floating heads of death, and other routine activities here at our house, my kids don't fear many things. That is, however, NOT the same thing as being ignorant to the dangers. Our pool has an automatic pool cover that I personally, at one-eighth of a ton, have chased my 150 pound Rottweiler across the top of. It's always closed unless an adult is out at the pool super-vising. All of my kids start swim lessons at the age of one and con-tinue to this day. As an additional safety factor, we frequently watch cartoons about mermaids. I've really got this safety thing covered.

Have I ever dropped a baby at the pool? In euphemisms, the answer is a resounding YES, but as far as actual failure to catch a recently hurled small human being, the answer is an emphatic NO. But what would happen if I did? Well, not much. The kid would can-nonball wildly into the pool where I would retrieve them instantly before judging them on style points. Out of the four kids we have had, we still have three of them. It's hard to argue with a 75% safety record. I think I know what I'm talking about.

So how many times have I actually had to "save" a kids life? Geez, I don't know. Maybe five? Six? I don't remember for sure. I can, how-ever, tell you that those figures are probably no joke. As redneck as the causes may be, or as heroic as "saving a human life" may be, it pretty much happens all the time when you have, or are around, kids or other stupid people. I'm sorry, I didn't mean stupid. I meant uneducated.

There really is no better experience than teachers. No..wait...I think I've got that backwards. Well, whatever, I think maybe it does work both ways. The goal is to teach people...but preferably through statistically SURVIVABLE experiences.

Just yesterday, I was explaining to my oldest daughter, while turning around to check her seatbelt before jumping the construction site, why it is that I won't let her and her friends ride their bicycles around our neighborhood without me. The obvious answer is that none of MY friends will ride bikes with me, but there is also that underlying fear that some psycho in a panel van is gonna steal my kid when I'm not there. This kind of fear is precisely why I don't mind throwing my kid in the pool. I KNOW I'll catch her because, well....I simply don't know how to let go.

That's probably the hardest thing for a parent to do. One of these days I am going to have to stop catching my kid in the pool. When will that be? I don't know. One seems a little young. Heck, even eight seems young. God willing, I'll drop dead in about ten years, leaving them with just enough "teaching" to live "safely" on the edge and just enough insurance money to hire a good band to play their pool parties, and I'll never have to worry about it. But if that doesn't happen, I've got some decisions to make. I've been eyeballing a new sniper rifle too, so maybe that allegedly "unsupervised" bike ride around the block isn't as far off as she thinks.

I guess the answer to the question of "when do you stop catching the babies you threw?" is....

Never. You just learn to make the net a little harder to see.

Shots IN a liquor store.

One of my favorite quotes is from a local guy that owned a junkyard. Just above his shooting trophies, he posted a sign for all of his customers to see. The sign said "If you steal from me, don't bother running. You'll just die tired". Obviously, I always loved that quote. But it reminded me of one of my other favorite stories from good ol' Indianapolis.

When I was barely 21, a good buddy of mine made his first visit home to Indianapolis since enlisting in the Marine Corps. I picked him up when he arrived in town and asked him what he wanted to do first. He replied, without hesitation, "I need beer and I need porn". Lucky for him, I was a heathen and knew where to get both in one easy stop.

There was a liquor store on East Washington street that I frequented for two reasons, and neither of them related to alcohol. You can buy alcohol anywhere. But in Indianapolis in 1992, there was only one place you could see the dynamic duo of liquor store employees "Jim and Bubba" in action, and it was also the ONLY place that still had seemingly knee-high shag carpet left over from the psychedelic days of the 70's. Who could resist that?

Jim and Bubba were Beavis and Butthead before Beavis and Butthead existed. There may have been one living brain cell shared between the two of them. They lived together in an apartment they called "the Bakery", and it didn't get its name for making pastries. The two of them smelled like Spicoli's van even in a 10,000 square foot building with 30 year old musty shag carpet. I have no idea who thought to put them in charge of running a serious business. Obviously it wasn't the best idea because the store is long gone now.

But on this particular day, I knew I could score my buddy a boobie-book and some cold beer while simultaneously blowing his mind with the ten-inch deep shag carpet. We HAD to go there. As a friend, I owed him this experience.

We entered the store and walked immediately to the counter where Bubba was reading a dirty magazine. I greeted him and informed him of my friends request. Bubba sent him directly to the magazine rack, made an immediate suggestion to "open the third book from the left on shelf number two to page 54".

"Now turn it sideways", Bubba said, without even looking up from his own smutty book. The next thing he said caused me to throw up in my mouth a little bit and I've not eaten a Roast Beef sandwich again since that day.

It was then that it occurred to me that we had walked into the store without needing a machete to carve a path.

"Hey Bubba", I said, "What happened to the shag carpet?!?!?!"

"Oh...yeah dude...", Bubba answered, still without looking up from his magazine. "We got robbed."

I stood confused and temporarily silent before asking the obvious question...

"Somebody stole your carpet?"

"Naw man", Bubba answered, finally interested enough to look at me. "Some old boy pulled a gun on Jimmy last week".

"No kidding?", I responded. "What happened?"

Bubba finally seemed genuinely interested in our new conversation and became slightly animated, acting out the scenes of his forthcoming story with typical fat, stoner guy, enthusiasm...

"Ol' Boy walks in here, picks up a six-pack of Stroh's, sets it on the counter and lays a 5-dollar bill beside it. Jimmy opens the register to make change, and Ol' Boy sticks a 22 in Jimmy's face and says 'Gimme all that money'"

"Is that when he took the carpet?", I asked.

"Naw bro. My boy Jimmy drops to the floor behind the counter and pops back up with his .357 and puts two rounds right in Ol' Boys face."

"Okay", I respond, still focused on my original line of questioning... "How does this relate to the missing carpet?"

"Oh....", said Bubba, as he lost complete interest and delved back into his porn. "We couldn't get Ol' Boys head out of the carpet."

"Geez!", I responded, finally impressed. "That's terrible!".

"Naaaah", Bubba answered totally casually and completely lost in porn by this point..."We kept that dudes five bucks".

And that is why I loved Jimmy and Bubba's liquor store.

Lucky

There is a little park in Indiana that used to be mostly run by bikers. I went there once when my brothers band played a biker rally. I actually signed a waiver to enter, in front of armed biker guards, stating that they would not be liable for my death. It didn't say accidental death...just death. Basically, I signed a permission slip to be murdered. It didn't seem like that bad of an idea at the time because I was young and stupid then, as opposed to being old and stupid now. No one calls it old and stupid though because if you live past young and stupid without learning anything at all, they just call you "lucky". This is ironic because I met a biker at this particular event named "Lucky". I'm not making this up.

After introducing himself to me with the casual icebreaker of "Hey man, you wanna join the KKK?", "Lucky" offered his name and a swig from his whiskey bottle....both of which I graciously declined. About an hour later, "Lucky" beat a rival biker named "Ace" to death not five feet away from me with a large metal police issue flashlight. If things had been different and "Ace" had killed "Lucky", they would have had to bury him under whatever his "Christian name" might have been, although, I don't suspect that wording was appropriate here. You simply can't have a tombstone that says: "Here lies Lucky. He was beaten to death". It's totally cool for a guy named Ace though.

Anyway, you never really forget witnessing your first brutal murder so I've always remembered that place and that special fellow named "Lucky". I don't know if Lucky is still alive or not but the park is still doing just fine. Last Sunday, I was at work at my new location which is about a mile from that quaint little Indiana park. Funny thing is, I see more Amish people in horse-drawn buggies than I do bikers on Harleys. My store was full of Amish people and 7th Day Adventists on this particular day, along with a few young half-naked teenagers that had been swimming in the park, so when a distinct rumbling in the parking lot began to rattle the windows, I immediately recognized the sounds. I grabbed the microphone for the store intercom and shouted "Attention Amish people! I can hear your horses farting outside! Do NOT let them poop in my parking lot!"

But alas I was wrong. It wasn't gassy horses at all. It was about 80 Harley-Davidsons carrying a large group of bikers. Not just any bikers either...it was the Florida chapter of the same "Club" that I watched murder a man the last time I saw them in this town. Old hippies will tell you that "Flashbacks are neat...because they're free", but not all flashbacks are good. Large posses of murderers meet the "not-good" flashback criteria...for me anyway.

The first biker entered the store and came straight to me. He was a large man who appeared to be in his 40's. He wore no shirt and a black leather vest covered in patches proclaiming his affiliations and his dedication to being a 1%'er. The vest appeared to have not been removed in a decade or better. It was very dirty but it was not recent dirt. In fact, the vest, much like the man himself, appeared to not be covered in accumulated dirt so much as it appeared to be the actual origin of dirt. The man beneath the vest was equally leathery and dark, and rather than just having filth intricately woven into his skin, he appeared to actually be leaking motor oil from some of his pores. The lifestyle wasn't just running through his veins, it was seeping through his flesh.

His hands were visibly scarred from what I presume was decades of bug killing at high speeds and his knuckles had become fossilized outlines of the shapes of some of the larger insects along with what appeared to be old scars inflicted by the teeth of some equally unfortunate humans. Even standing still, the man's hands vibrated with what I assume was habitual and conditioned response to years of clenching his rumbling road horse. He looked like a dirty Terminator with just a touch of Parkinson's Disease...but still mean enough to kill you with his eyes alone. Just in case his eyes were not in the mood for killing, he wore a huge buck knife strapped to his hip and what appeared to be a pistol poorly concealed on the back-side of his vest. He was the real deal. He wasn't going back to his lake house to park the bike and start another dull week at the accounting firm. But for now, he was just standing silently before me, staring intently at my left hand..... which happened to be covered in fluorescent green bandages with pink hearts on them, courtesy of my six-year old daughter.

The biker looked at my hand for what seemed like an eternity before looking me square in the eye, and saying: "Cute Band-Aid". He didn't smile. He wasn't being funny. I think he sincerely wanted to punch me for being the biggest sissy he had seen in the last 1000 miles. As a general rule though, I don't fight customers, especially those of the armed Terminator variety that bring an actual army to my business. Instead of responding that I had just mangled my finger to the bone in a power saw accident and trying to salvage some "street cred", I made the less wise decision to look him back in the eye, and reply with my best forced confidence: "Thank you. I have the matching panties."

It was an uncalculated risk, at best, but it was also a response that he was surely not prepared for. We did not speak again but he did not move for a honest five minutes and although I dared not look him in the eye again, I could feel the heat of his stare for the entire 300 seconds that it lasted. I resisted the urge to wink at him and say "Did I just blow your mind man?", only because of my certainty that he would stab my face repeatedly, right there in front of the Amish people...and on this particular day, I had ZERO desire to be "rushed" to the hospital in a horse and buggy.

It was at this point, for whatever reason, that it occurred to me that there are fewer and fewer things in this world that I don't pass off as "normal". For example, why was I in a gas station with Amish people and a mob of leather clad death merchants on a Sunday afternoon? I don't have a clue. It's funny that this year I manage a truck stop, last year I managed a restaurant, and the years before that I flew airplanes. Apparently, I too am on a road trip. Mine is on the grander scale of life than just a trip down the highway though. Maybe I don't have a club of raggedy renegade comrades, and maybe I brush my teeth instead of shellacking them black with the glossy carbon of weeks worth of motorcycle exhaust, but maybe me and this oily leathery bastard before me aren't so different. Sure he probably rapes and murders people sometimes and probably deals in illegal goods to provide funding for his continual quests, but once you get beyond those minor details, we are both just tourists here.

I envy my friends who have seriously long term, developed careers, carved out of years of passionate and relentless pursuit of an unwavering goal in a specific field of study. I love that some people read trade magazines in their spare time because it's part of who they are. I'm just not that guy. I never have been. I've never had that "destination". I'm just a drifter. In a society where your work defines so much of your being, my never having a "professional identity" has left me with a bit of an identity crisis. If not work, what exactly is defining me? Where is my spot in the universe? What will I be when I grow up?

It's too late for those thoughts now. Life, statistically, is half over for me. "Growing up" probably isn't in the cards. This week, my goal is to make a functional volcano with my kids because it's neat. Next week, I want to perfect my front flip in to the pool. This year, I need to finish getting my first book published. Next year I want to have a sculpture exhibition somewhere. In between, I need to spend 60 hours a week running a business in bizarro land, and actually digging it, because it's a stop on my journey. I'm going to restore another boat, probably get my CDL and never use it, repaint my bathroom, wonder how my kids keep getting older every time I blink, and continue to not really have a plan. My experience with road trips has been that getting lost is 100% of the fun.

Sometimes, if you're really lucky, you'll have a clear idea of where you are going in life. People like me will envy you. Sometimes, if you are even luckier, you'll just keep putting gas in the tank and turning corners and still probably end up someplace pretty cool. Sadly, if you are the genuine "Lucky", you'll just get crazy drunk in the park and kill a dude. That's probably not nearly as cool, but hey, we've all got our roads to travel.

Happy motoring.

...and non-motoring if you're Amish.

In 1971, a legend was born

I just bought a comic book that I've spent several years looking for. That's a pretty dumb thing to do for a guy at my advanced age of almost 800 years. It's one of those things that will make my wife shake her head. Occasionally, though, even I have intent.

The comic book I bought is an old French comic called "Dan Cooper". More people than not have no idea who Dan Cooper is. In twenty to fifty more years, almost no one will know who Dan Cooper is. More interesting yet, is that even the people who are familiar with Dan Cooper now, have no idea who Dan Cooper is. That's what makes Dan Cooper a legend.

It doesn't seem like that long ago that I was a kid, until I reflect back on it. I played Cowboys and Indians with my friends...because that's what kids did before video games. That's right, we didn't have video games and we didn't have internet either. We had books, played outside, and we were told bedtime stories. We learned about legends. In my short time on this Earth, all that has changed. John Wayne is not the idol of American kids anymore. I'm not sure if anyone is. I sound like my Grandpa now, and that's not a bad thing.

In 1971, three months after I was born, a man boarded a Northwest Orient Airlines 727, flight 305, carrying a black attaché case. The name on his ticket read "Dan Cooper". The flight was supposed to be a non-eventful 30 minute flight from Portland, Oregon to Seattle, Washington. That flight made Dan Cooper a legend.

After lighting a cigarette and ordering a bourbon, Mr. Cooper slipped the flight stewardess a note that said he had a bomb and was hijacking the airplane. Hours later, after landing, refueling, and collecting a $200,000 ransom and a parachute, the 727 took off again headed for Reno Nevada. When the plane landed in Reno, Mr. Cooper was no longer on board. No one was injured and the culprit has never been seen or heard from again, mostly because Mr. Cooper never existed. To this day, there is only one unsolved airplane hijacking in American History. The man who did it is called Dan Cooper, or D.B. Cooper, which was an alias he stole from a French Comic book.

Do I idolize Dan Cooper? A thief? A hijacker? A liar? No.

Do I miss that part of American history? Will I be sad when all the "legends" are forgotten? Yes. Billy the Kid, Dan Cooper, and John Wayne are all legends who will probably follow no-names like me into obscurity someday. But they made life exciting for a while. They fueled dreams and built the mystique of America.

People might ask if I need to hang a picture on the wall in order to be reminded to seize each day and make it legendary. The answer is yes. Yes I do. I have a television now, and video games, and internet. I have a million things to distract me. Now I have one more thing on my wall to remind me to always take those leaps of faith that make life legendary. I don't plan to hijack an airplane, I already have a pilot's license. But someday, I just might do something special, maybe even legal. When I do, I'll give a subtle nod to Dan Cooper, whoever that is.

This might be the tequila talking....

Somehow, despite my intentional lack of exercise since the late 1900's, I have managed to acquire a condition known as "athlete's foot". So I was putting the "over the counter" cream on my foot and, for reasons that could have my man card revoked, I read the directions. Not that I didn't know HOW to apply a cream to my feet, it's just that I found it unfathomably odd that there WERE directions on how to apply cream to my feet. How many options can there really be?

Step One....squirt all cream onto newly carpeted floor

Step Two....dance in it until you feel sweet relief.

Anyway, it's not the directions that bothered me, it was the warning. The tiny box that contained my tiny tube of medicine for my FEET actually warned me not to get the cream on my vagina. Yes, you read that correctly. Obviously, there are a great number of issues here, but because I'm tired, I'm only going to focus on two of them.

1. I was not aware that I had my own vagina. And after I finish this note, I plan to spend the rest of my evening searching for it.

2. How exactly does this manufacturer think I am going to get FOOT medicine into my VAGINA? Obviously, it has been a problem in the past or there would not be a warning on the box now.

The second point there actually brings me back to my first issue, which was how to apply the foot cream. Maybe I HAVE been doing this all wrong. Maybe there is another application method that other people use that I have not been made aware of.

Revised application of foot cream process:

Step One: Apply foot cream medication to the nearest vagina you can find.

Step Two: Using your bare feet, kick the vagina applicator repeatedly until you feel relief in your feet.

Side note: Be careful not to get foot cream INSIDE the vagina, by using a series of short, non-invasive kicks.

WHAT HAVE I BEEN MISSING ALL OF THESE YEARS??????

I understand the concept of product liability. I understand that the manufacturer of my lawn mower actually has to put a note on the mower reminding me not to stick my hands or feet into the quickly spinning sharpened metal blade that is housed underneath a protective cover where any contact would HAVE to be intentional...but are we really getting to a point as a society that next year my lawn mower will have to have a posted warning telling me not to stick my vagina into the blades?

I went to the always trustworthy internet to seek answers and found something that I once knew but had simply forgotten. Athlete's Foot is the same fungal infection as "Jock itch" . Which actually does help explain things a little bit. I can see this medicine being applied for jock itch and then somehow finding its way to a vagina being a more likely prospect than worrying about some barefoot hillbilly with Athletes foot kicking you in your vagina.

As all things do, my internet research presented me with a new issue. If Jock itch and Athletes Foot are the same fungus, can't we call them something different to avoid this kind of confusion?

I played a lot of sports in high school, and that usually gets people the label of being a "Jock". However, despite my repeated attempts and requests, at no point in ANY of those sports did my coaches or officials allow me to involve my penis in the contest. I was however, allowed to use my FEET in every event. So I think JOCK FEET might be a better name for that particular condition, brought on by sports. However, problems arise yet again when you go referring to your severe pelvic itch as "Athletes Itch", because again, that would seem to imply that your penis should be receiving a Varsity Letter Jacket. Not likely. So obviously we can't just interchange the names of these two similar conditions.

I don't think there is anything wrong with simply marketing a product called Foot Itch medicine. It's simple, to the point, and I suspect, will reduce the chances of it ending up in anyone's vagina. Even if someone actually does have a 12 inch penis, they still aren't likely to buy a product called "Foot Itch Medicine" to stop that wiener from itching. That would be not only stupid, but also arrogant. Which brings me to another addition of my now spiraling out of control tequila fueled rant...if we just switched to the metric system like the rest of the world, the 12 inches and foot thing would never cross paths again. But I digress...

So what do we call the medicine for your itchy scrotum? How about nothing at all. It needs no fancy product name or advertisement. You don't see commercials for different kinds of crutches because some things just sell themselves on sheer necessity. Itchy ball medicine is one of those things. Just walk into any pharmacy, point to your man parts and say "It itches." The pharmacists most likely will NOT give you "foot itch medication". Problem solved. Everyone goes home happy and drunk guys don't go to bed wondering if they really have a vagina that no one told them about.

Like I said, this might just be the tequila talking...

I want you...to want me

As you may recall, if you are one of the three people who read my constant ramblings, I was the proud recipient of a state sponsored certificate of recognition honoring my apparently "excessive" speed on one of the states newly paved highways back in February of this year. It was three o'clock in the morning on a Tuesday when a State Police Officer/ Super Ninja was able to hide under a bridge in a black patrol car and single me, the only car in a five mile stretch in either direction, out and recognize me as a danger to myself and others. It is absolutely true that I was going 75 MPH in a 55MPH zone so I cannot say that I was entirely undeserving of his attention.

However, like most cops who became cops because they want to seek revenge and get some sense of restored pride from all of the mean bullies from their cruel high school days, this one came straight of the academy with a serious chip on his shoulder. He greeted me with, "How much have you had to drink tonight?" and to which I replied, "I'm fine sir, how are you?" He immediately restated his question more politely by yelling it instead of asking it. "I asked you how much have you had to drink tonight?"

"Not a drop", I said, "I just got off work. Hence, this stylish uniform. I'm just going home"

"Don't you think you are going a little fast through here?" asked the officer in his best tough guy voice.

I didn't answer immediately. Instead I looked up ahead at the completely empty 4 lane wide newly paved highway, and the turned around to look behind us at the, again, totally empty four lane wide newly paved highway and paused again, for effect. I tried to raise one eyebrow inquisitively, which totally pisses me off because I can't do it and instead I just end up raising both eyebrows and looking completely surprised, which is completely NOT the effect I was going for, but anyway, I finally answered: "Apparently so".

I gave him my license and registration and he went back to his car to write me a citation for my heinous crime. I waited patiently and he returned after some ten or fifteen minutes with the written proof of my sin. He held the ticket down at his side while he took the opportunity to lecture me. "I see you haven't had a ticket since 1992". (Technically, that is false, I've had 13 tickets since 1992 but I have beaten every single one of them in court or done diversion programs so they don't show up on my record.) "But guess what? You are getting a ticket tonight", he said proudly.

Whatever. This was like the twentieth ticket I've had in my life so I don't exactly stress out over them anymore.

Then I looked at the ticket. He wrote me up for EXACTLY 75 MPH in a 55 MPH, knowing full well that the price break on tickets is 74 MPH. Awesome.

"So how much is this one?", I asked after turning the ticket over and NOT seeing the price that had been clearly listed on the back of the ticket like it was on every single one of the last 19 I had received.

"I don't know. They've updated the whole process now on computers so you'll have to log on to the website and look it up", replied the officer.

Whatever. "Cool. Thanks." THIS, was apparently what the officer meant by "updating the process".

I went home and logged on the computer to see how much my fine was. My ticket "had not been processed" yet so I was unable to get ANY information at all. I checked again the next day. Still nothing. The next day...still nothing. I put the ticket on a shelf and forgot about it. I have A.D.D.. They should be happy I tried for three days.

Fast forward 65 days. I get a letter in the mail informing me that I have failed to comply with my court date and that my license was now suspended. I would need to call the courts, not the BMV, to resolve the issue. So the next day, I called the courts...pretty much every hour all day. I got voicemail every time saying they were "experiencing a high volume of calls and to try my call again later". This went on for a few days before I put the letter up on the shelf, with my ticket, and forgot about it. It's not like my A.D.D. was suddenly cured by having a suspended license.

Another month goes by and happen to uncover the letters while looking for something completely unrelated. "Oh yeah. I should do something about this." Then I set the letter back down and went back to looking for whatever it was I had lost that day.

Last night, it occurred to me, while talking to a friend, that I haven't had a valid driver's license for a few months. Honestly, I kind of dig that. I'm sticking it to man. I'm in NO hurry at all at this point. I'm a criminal. I'm BAD.

So I went to traffic court today. But it wasn't there. They moved it. "Over at Washington Street and Franklin Road", I was told. So I drove around the area for a while and didn't see anything resembling a court. I call information from my cell phone and receive the old invalid address, which was totally helpful. I understand that I'm probably the only person in this city of over one million who's needed to go to traffic court in the 10 months since the last phone book came out.

Whatever. I keep looking. I see nothing. I phone a friend. "No clue", he said.

I finally just started literally driving past every single store front in the area. I see no signs for a traffic court. However, I do find one place with no sign at all, but it's in a strip mall between a ghetto-ass Chuck-E Cheese and a seemingly vacant spot with a "New Life Church" banner hanging from the roof. Realizing this is probably a justifiable place for a group of cops, I roll down the window and ask a sad looking dude sitting on the curb, "Excuse me sir, is this the traffic court?".

"Yep", he said. Sweet.

I park and go inside. I'm stopped immediately by a fairly serious looking security station and metal detector. I ask the cops working that checkpoint "Any chance of anyone ever updating 411 or maybe putting a sign on this place?"

"Yeah, I'm not sure who's job that is", said the cop. Apparently, it's no ones job.

So I take off my belt and empty my pockets and pretend I'm trying to board a plane. I pass the through the metal detector and accidentally left my car keys in the little security tray, which no one noticed.

I got my number and waited in a non-existent line, which wasn't entirely surprising since no one in the city knows this secret club-house even exists, and was called up pretty quickly. The girl at the window clearly hated her job/life and asked me "What do you want?". I pushed my letters from the state through the security window to her and said, "You sent me these last month, and I'm guessing I need to do something about them".

"I'd say you certainly do sir. Do you realize that your license is suspended for failure to pay and that you've missed your court date? Sir, you can be arrested at any time for this. Do you realize that?"

Awesome, I thought to myself. I am a wanted man. I am soooo bad. This feels great. Maybe I should leave now and pay it later.

"Sir, you need to pay this TODAY", she said. "Seriously, the police WILL arrest you and you WILL go to jail", she said. I think she was attempting to frighten me with the threat of losing my freedom. She did frighten me, with the realization that the police outnumber like 30,000 to 1, and they have had my address for over two months, along with my license plate information, a picture of me, and a description of my car. And yet somehow, this highly trained task force had failed to capture me, the dangerous criminal. Why, armed with every conceivable piece of information, did they fail to capture me? Because they don't care. What I did was nothing more than an opportunity to collect tax money. This angers me. Because it totally devalues my feelings of being a true criminal. It felt good to be "wanted". It felt sad to realize that they only wanted me if stumbled into their way someday when there was nothing else to do. I wasn't Billy the Kid on a WANTED poster at the post office, I was the ugly girl standing alone in the bar at closing time hoping someone would notice. Dammit. Not cool.

So I paid the fine. The lady then informs me that it will take "at least five days" before the BMV receives the information that I have now paid my fine and has a chance to review my file for license reinstatement. Seriously. Now that we have "updated the process with computers", it will take at least five days for the information to reach a fellow state agency located not 10 miles from where I was paying the fine. Impressive.

"Technically", said the lady as I walked away, "your license remains suspended and you can still be arrested if you get caught driving".

"Thanks!" I shouted back to the lady as I reached the security station again to exit. "Excuse me sir, would you mind handing me my car keys?"

Then I jaywalked back to my car and drove off illegally...totally depressed. I almost called them back to tell them about the dead hooker in the trunk of my car, but I realized I'd just get a busy signal.

What's got two thumbs and gives great advice?

I don't think I'm particularly expert when it comes to being an expert on surviving animal attacks but the fact that I'm not dead yet certainly lends some credence to my potential. I once met a man who had been severely mauled by a "pet" bear and he lost a leg, an ear, and part of his arm. He tried to convince me that the animal itself was not that dangerous but that he had made a "human error" in handling the animal. I leaned in towards his missing ear and gently whispered "Somehow you don't seem like a credible source for judging animal instinct". Maybe it's just me.

Regardless of my complete lack of technical qualifications, the fact that I can still point to myself with both of my own thumbs inspires me to share some of what I have learned and to compare those possible wives tales with theories that I actually believe to be true. So here is some advice that will either save your life or get you killed. I feel comfortable sharing it because I know I'll only get feedback from the people it saves and thus, I can continue to feel smart. Contrarily, if my advice does kill you and you do find yourself able to reach out to me from beyond the grave to dispute me, please don't. You are no Patrick Swayze.

Okay, since I've already mentioned bears, we can start with bear attacks. If a Grizzly bear attacks you, you are supposed to lie motionless and take it until the bear grows weary of shredding your flesh and simply wanders off to take a nap. I know that sounds a little like prison sex but they say it's your best bet for survival. However, if you are attacked by a BLACK bear, you are supposed to try to scare it away by yelling and flailing your arms and trying to appear "big". Black bears are apparently bluffers and will supposedly retreat if you stand up to them.

The problem with this advice is obvious. If you are colorblind, attacked at night, or simply don't know a damn thing about bears (like 99% of the world), you now have a 50% chance of doing the VERY wrong thing. From what I hear you don't want to intentionally box a Grizzly bear or be the only person you know to be unnecessarily raped by a Black bear. Until the park rangers start making the bears wear glow in the dark nametags, you are taking a pretty big chance by responding in any fashion at all.

My advice for surviving bear attacks is simple. Either carry a gun or always travel with someone much slower and who consistently reeks of fish sticks. There really is no other good advice here.

The problem with similar animals who respond differently in attack situations reminds of a time my cousin was being attacked by bees (a baseball bat to a large nest may or may not have inspired this war). I recall running into his house and yelling to his older brother "Come quick! He's being attacked by bees!!!!" The response was typical of older, and yet still immature, brothers. He just looked up at me and said, "What kind of bees?"

Even in my inquisitive youth, when the bees attacked, I never once thought to stop running and ask them what kind of bees they were. Frankly, I don't see responding differently in the instance of a bear attack. Unlike bears, and despite the curiosity of said older brothers, it really doesn't matter what kind of bee attacks you because the defense you employ will be exactly the same. RUN! Run as far and as fast as you can. Immediately. Cover your nose and mouth while you do it. Don't run away screaming "Hey! What kind of bees are you?" with your mouth open. You will die.

Most bees will stop chasing you after 600 feet. African Killer bees will chase you up to a half mile though. So if you are fat, like me, you are either going to die from the stings or from trying to run a half mile. So if you are some kind of nerdy entomologist who can immediately distinguish an African Killer bee from a normal bee, you are probably fat and out of shape too so you might as well just lie down and die well rested because, clearly, death was God's plan for you.

Alligator attacks are somewhat of a specialty to me and I do consider myself to be an authority on this one. Mostly because we don't have alligators in Indiana, I can say pretty much anything I want here and most of my friends won't know the difference. In the event of an alligator attack, you should taunt the creature with large chunks of raw meat, while hula dancing.

Okay, maybe that's not true, but it isn't much sillier than the advice that is commonly dispensed by so called "experts". There are three things you are traditionally told to do in the event of a gator attack. The first is to RUN. That shouldn't be hard to remember and actually is EXTREMELY good advice. Alligators can only run short distances, because they are heavy smokers, and also can't run more than 10MPH. If you find yourself ever being chased by this carnivorous modern day dinosaur I think you will be pleasantly surprised to find that you can run faster than that for an equally short distance. The inadvertent pooping of yourself will also provide additional obstacles to the ensuing gator.

A MAJOR point of contention amongst advisors of gator attacks is whether or not run in a straight line or to zig zag. The zig zagging theory was popularized because of alligators alleged lack of peripheral vision but later it was revealed that the zig zag theory was just started by a fairly slow guy who wanted to give himself a decent crack at survival against his much quicker friends. Running in a straight line is the right thing to do. The shortest distance between two SAFE points is a straight line. The shortest distance between life and death is a zig zag line. Remember that, even when your fat friend tells you otherwise.

The second piece of popular advice for fending off a gator attack applies to times when outrunning the gator is not an option. Experts say that you should mount the alligators back and press his head to the ground so that he cannot tear you into tiny delicious pieces. Poke him in the eyes while you are at it. Seriously.

The problem I see with this advice is, again, fairly obvious. At no point in these instructions does it tell you when to stop riding the pissed off alligator. To me, the time to safely dismount the now EXTREMELY pissed and even MORE hungry alligator would be.... never. I believe that all alligator rides are either eternal or until the alligator expires from natural causes, like old age.

The third and I presume, very final, piece of advice for fighting an alligator is applicable only when the alligator has succeeded in dragging you into the water. You are supposed to punch the alligator in his snout until he releases you. I have no opinion on this one simply because I don't know anyone who has ever tried it. If you do it, let me know how that works out.

Alligator attacks are obviously not likely. What is much more likely is simply being attacked by a dog. Most dog attacks can be prevented by using common sense and not provoking or frightening a dog and by not trying to snack on his dinner. If you encounter an unfamiliar dog, do not make eye contact or smile. Both are considered signs of aggression. Do not turn and run, that is considered weakness and can provoke attack. They say you should gently extend a hand and let the dog sniff you out and familiarize itself with you.

I'm torn on the extension of hand advice. I've had unfamiliar dogs try to "familiarize" themselves with me before and the dog NEVER started with my hand. I've had dogs use their noses to lift me up by the groin like a floor jack before, but never just sniff my hand. Obviously they are more curious to sniff out your genitals but under NO CIRCUMSTANCES do you want to greet an unfamiliar dog by extending your genitals for his or her sniffing pleasure. Bad things can happen man. BAD THINGS. The only good advice for fending off an attacking dog is to either keep a pocket full of quickly dispensable "feeder" kittens, or to taze the dog until he pees out of his own eyes.

Realistically though, I like dogs more than I like people so if a dog attacks you, I probably won't help. It's natural selection. God's will. Fate. Whatever you want to call it. Odds are, the dog is probably just going to molest your leg for a while and move on. If that happens, it's best not to tell anyone. Just go home, wash your pants, and learn from it.

If you are ever attacked by a monkey, my only request is that you have someone film it. That shit cracks me up. hope this helps. Thank you and God Bless.

Your friend,

"Two Thumbs" Garrett.

Noteworthy day

I was at the truck stop today (technically, it was actually considered a "travel center" because it did not have hookers) and a big passenger bus stopped in to let all the passengers off to spring leaks and then refill themselves. A swarm of women ran to the ladies room in a panicky huddle. Moments later, one of them emerged with a young baby. I am pretty sure she had the baby before she went in there though. Anyway, she only got about 50 feet away from the bathroom before she stopped suddenly, perked up a bit, and then went scrambling back to the bathroom. Knowing that sometimes a good performance essentially demands a sequel, I thought nothing of her seemingly immediate encore.

However, the woman emerged from the bathroom again just as quickly, and this time, even more panicky. I was the closest person to her and she immediately called out to me. "Did you see anyone just leave this bathroom with a grey purse?", she asked.

Hmmmmm.....I thought to myself. I saw a woman with one breast seemingly larger than the other, one lady that looked exactly like Ozzy Osbourne, and one girl that I think was a dwarf. As a guy, that's pretty much all I'm trained to notice. A gray purse is not something that would stand out to me. I wanted to be a wise guy and say, "No girl, but did you see the shoes on that last woman??? Mmmm... mmm...mmm....they did NOT go with that skirt child" But that would have not only seemed immensely gay, but also probably would have irritated this already freaked out young mother.

It didn't take long to put her situation into perspective. She appeared to be about 20 years old, with a baby not more than three months old, and it was just the two of them. She was in a small town in Indiana, a little more than half way between her home in Chicago and her destination in Cincinnati. Suddenly, she had NO money, no credit cards, no ID, no cell phone, no ANYTHING, except a crying baby. And to make matters worse, her bus was scheduled to leave in five minutes. What could she do? Go to Cincinnati penniless, without a phone, ID, or anything else? Or stay in a small town in the middle of no where hoping to find a purse that was likely already out of the building or empty in a dumpster, and then have no way to get anywhere else at all? The reason for her panic was certainly understandable.

Word spread quickly and everyone in the building began checking trash cans and anywhere else they could think to look. The bus driver came in and looked too. The young girl knew it was stolen. She sat the purse down to change her baby's diaper and when she was finished her purse was gone. She borrowed a phone and immediately called the police. The bus was due to leave. The police would likely show up in a hour or so and say "sorry ma'am" and then file a report and leave. I had seen it happen many times.

The bus driver asked me who else was in the building before the bus arrived. I told him that there were maybe four male truck drivers, and a handful of employees present before the 50 or so people got off the bus. He asked me "So you think it was somebody on bus?".

"Sir, it certainly seems to be the case", I said.

"Well then", he said, "this bus ain't goin nowhere."

I liked this guy.

The building was loaded with security cameras but obviously none INSIDE the bathroom. Still, tapes were immediately reviewed and it was clear that no one had entered the bathroom in the ten minutes before the bus arrived. Then five women from the bus entered the bathroom together and left about the same time. The purse was then missing. Fifty suspects had just been narrowed down to four, as there was great confidence that the young mother had not stolen her own purse.

The sheriff showed up and I could tell he was going to take a report, wish her well, and go on his way. He too realized that this girl was in an especially bad circumstance and had a change of heart. He asked to review the tapes too. Then he went out and asked the four women to get off the bus. He searched each of them. I was impressed.

While this was happening, the young girl was still inside the building...crying and wondering what had gone astray in the world. The rest of us wondered too. It was one of those moments were you could actually see a collective loss of faith in humanity.

Then something wonderful happened. A truck driver handed the young woman a twenty dollar bill. She tried to refuse it but he simply smiled and walked away. Several other truck drivers immediately offered her rides in various directions, including her home in Chicago and her destination in Cincinnati. Meanwhile, the bus driver and 49 passengers waited, patiently and hopefully, for a positive outcome. An older employee of the sandwich shop inside the truck stop came over when she thought no one was looking and handed the young mother $12 and I heard her say "I'm so sorry dear, it's all I have". Again, the young mother tried to refuse it but the lady simply said "May God bless you and your baby" and returned to work.

Outside, the sheriff searched the third woman, and found the entire missing purse stuffed inside her bag. The woman who had stolen it had been sitting beside the young mother for the last 250 miles, talking to her, playing with her baby, and had even pretended to help look for the stolen purse. She knew perfectly well exactly who she was stealing from and what it was going to do to the young girl. Worse yet, she was planning to sit six inches away from her for another 200 miles and tell her how horrible it was that someone could do that to a young mother and her child. That is about as cold blooded as a person can be.

The young mother and her baby were able to once again board the bus, to a standing ovation, while the other woman was hand-cuffed and led away to spend the night in a small Indiana town jail. Justice was served. Everyone was excited to see the young mother was going to be okay and everyone was happy to see the offender be caught.

More importantly, I think, was that the day changed for every-one...not just the young mother. We had all lost a little hope for the world when this began. The young mother made one decision, not to be victim, and she called the police. The bus driver made one decision, not to let the only suspects get away. The officer made one decision, to go the extra mile and not just write a report. A truck driver made one decision, to see the young mother had cash to get through her next meal. Other truckers made one decision, to offer the young lady safe and free passage to her destination. An $8 an hour employee, who turned out to be a single mother of two, made one decision to give several post-tax hours of her wages to a stranger when she thought the girl need it even more than she did.

I had a front seat for the whole affair. Each person who thought they were discreetly trying to help was doing so under my watchful eye. It almost made me wonder if the entire thing hadn't been for my benefit. I was fully prepared to declare the decline and impending doom of civilization but instead I saw one disgusting act be trumped by seven other decent acts of genuine caring from complete stran-gers. It made me think that maybe there is hope for us yet.

All along, I had intended to help the young mother and never had to. Instead, I bought a $25 gas card and had a staff member give it to the restaurant worker who had selflessly given away her last $12. I wish it had been $2500 as I suspect she's probably just going to give it to someone else she deems more worthy anyway. Some people still do that kind of stuff.

Like I said, maybe there is hope for us all yet.

Thpeech

I'll be honest. I'm irritated by ALL medical terminology. It makes no sense. It is based on Latin language...which is interesting since even Latin people don't speak Latin.

I was interviewing a kid on Tuesday that had a speech impediment and he was trying to clarify that for me, as if it needed to be done. The whole time he was talking I was thinking how cruel it was to make someone with a speech impediment actually say those two words. He never actually did say them but he came close enough. Same goes for stutterers. I've long maintained that there should be at least three more "ers" on the end of that word.

Here's another idea....the right thing to call laryngitis is...nothing. It's a word that should ONLY exist in sign language.

Cardiac arrest? **Arrhythmia? Defibrillation** ? Wow! Totally unnecessary unless you need huge point scrabble words. If my doctor tells me I have "heart trouble" that's good enough. I'm not going to think he means I'm just incapable of love.

Erectile dysfunction? That sounds like something you'd have to worry about while building a bridge. The actual definition of "erectile" is: "capable of being raised into an upright position" . However if the handle breaks off of your favorite reclining chair while it's laid out flat and you can no longer raise the chair back up, I think we'd all agree that we would not profess the chair to now have "erectile dysfunction". We'd just say the chair was "broken" and if someone still wanted to use it, I guess they'd just have to lay down on it.

I recently had a phlebotomist explain to me that my poor dietary habits are "exacerbating" my high cholesterol. First of all, I didn't know what a phlebotomist even was. If I had to guess, based on breaking the word down into other words I knew, I would have guessed it was a spray bottle full of phlegm and not a person who takes my blood. But the actual etymology is "Vein cutter" which means if medical terminology ever drives you to slit your own wrists you can die with the knowledge that you are now, technically, a successful phlebotomist.

As for "exacerbating my high cholesterol", I think we can all agree that that just sounds dirty.

"Plantar fasciitis" was the reason I was recently given that my feet sometimes hurt in the morning. It sounds more like a destination on Star Trek than an explanation of anything I should actually understand. So I asked for that to be translated into layman's terms. P.S. a "layman" is "a person who is not considered an expert in a particular field of knowledge" and not merely "a man who lays" or "is incapable of being raised into an upright position". It's important to note that difference here. It's one thing to say to your doctor: "I'm sorry, could you please translate "plantar fasciitis for me, as I'm not an expert in this field of knowledge." but it's another thing to say, "Doc, I don't understand what you are saying because I have erectile dysfunction".

So my doctor said "You have a foot that's not working correctly".

I said "I know. I just told you I have erectile dysfunction. But why do my feet hurt?"

After a quick moment of emotional discomfort, my doctor said: "You know what really aggravates me? That comment of yours never would have happened if we used the metric system like the rest of the world".

I said: "Yeah dude, I know. That's how I feel about Latin."

Getting over it

One of the most amusing things to hear when someone is in the middle of a crisis is when they throw their hands up in the air and proclaim: "That's it! I AM OVER IT!". It's funny because you know they aren't actually "OVER" anything. They are still as hopelessly pinned to whatever wall as they were before they stopped to say this stupid phrase. I don't know why no one says "I'm UNDER it". Admitting it is the first step...

When you are young, you'll do nearly anything to impress your friends or a potential sweetie. If this weren't true we would never have had generations of young men with Beatles bowl haircuts, teenagers with mustaches, or girls hooker-walking around in heels they can't walk in. It's a tough way to live.

As you get older, you simply stop caring. You finally "get over it". There is no such thing as peer pressure after the age of 35. Hell, after 35, most of the time you can't even talk YOURSELF into doing things. It's funny how your life changes like that. At 14, a kid will kill himself because people at school made fun of his pants. At 35, you will go to the mailbox in a dress shirt and boxer shorts just because you stopped caring so long ago.

I recall living in fear of accidentally farting in class when I was in high school. But I recall going to a nursing home and counting the number of farts an 80 year-old man would let as he walked through the room. He sometimes would let a little fart between EVERY SINGLE step. I thought he was just old and I chalked it up to age and a failing body...faulty O-rings. Now that I'm older, I'm convinced he knew. It wasn't accidental at all. He just stopped caring. He was "over it". Or maybe farting was all the commentary he felt like I deserved. That is considered acceptable though, because he was old. But you don't wanna be that guy. It might seem like there is a definite joy and freedom to that, but there is also still danger in the idea of "getting over it".

The schoolyard bullies might have actually been your truest friends. Their delivery might have been wrong, as you aren't supposed to throw a kid into a locker or dunk his head in a toilet or hang his underwear from the flagpole just to send some minor message. But at least they usually gave you some clear idea of what to look out for.

Better yet, your grandpa can say something right to your face, at your own wedding, that would get a kid expelled from most schools these days, and grandpa can totally get away with it. It's all about delivery...and AGE. Your grandpa can grab a microphone and tell you that you are fat, or to stop touching sheep, or anything else he wants to say. If he tells you that your breath smells like the back door of a wet goat, you'll probably take that message to heart and maybe even start brushing your dang teeth again. And that is actually a service. He's saving you from future shame by shaming you harshly now.

That's what bullies' mess up. With bullies, the shaming over-shadows the message. It's like sending someone a singing telegram for their birthday. You won't remember the birthday song, you will just remember a giant ape showing up at your office and making you feel weird for a while. Instead of a big ape delivering the message you could just have your grandpa swing by your office, poke his head in, and say: "You're not a kid anymore. Grow up". Then, you'll actually remember the message.

The real key is finding middle ground. You need balance. You don't want a big ape pulling your underwear up and tying it to your eyelids but sometimes criticism and peer pressure aren't all that bad. You need to know, but you need to hear it in a way that makes sense.

Here's the real question...especially if you are over the age of 35...if you met you today, would you expect anyone to date you? Or promote you? Do you make ANY effort at all? Have you totally let yourself or your life go? Given up on your dreams, given up on fitting into your old pants, or given up on wearing pants at all?

If you've been in the same job or relationship for more than five years, do you still make the same effort that you gave when you first started? If you met them this week, and all of your actions from this week alone were the basis on whether or not they wanted to spend the rest of their lives with you, would it have been enough? I bet not.

That's because your grandpa is probably not alive anymore and the bullies are all in jail by now. So it's up to YOU to figure out that you have bad breath, poor choice in wardrobe, awkward social skills, and that playing Nintendo for 17 hours a day might not be the support your partners needs. It's up to you to remember to buy flowers, to EARN your paycheck, to comb your hair, to be a good neighbor, to make dinner, to say "thank you', "I'm sorry", or "I love you" like they were the most important words ever spoken, to open a door, and try to still be the fish your boss or your partner can proudly show people in other boats and say: "Hey, check out what I caught".

And if you don't do that, no one is likely to come stuff you in the locker or stick your head in the toilet. They are just going to take your job, steal your lover, and generally make you wish they had only run your underwear up the flagpole. There are a lot of people out there, long after high school, that still want to eat your lunch. I'm just saying school is never really out.

I miss my grandpa...and when he died I remember someone commenting to my dad: "Life goes on, but you never really get over it." At the time I thought they were just talking about losing grandpa. It took me about 30 more years to figure that one out.

As life goes on, you'd better not get over it.

A box and chocolate milk

Perhaps the earliest childhood memory I have is being disappointed that my mother wasn't black. Not that I didn't love my mother. I did. It's just that somehow, I had been misguided into thinking that chocolate milk came from chocolate women, and that was what I wanted. I'm being absolutely serious.

In high school, my friend Matt and I discussed buying an abandoned gas station to live in. We thought it would be cool, and probably cheaper and less of a smoking hazard than trying to rent out a functional and currently operating gas station. I think part of the allure was having your friends over to drink beer in your crappy old gas station and then when they finally had to pee, they'd ask to use your bathroom. You'd say "Sure, no problem. Go outside and look for the door. The key is hanging up on the wall here...attached to a giant broomstick so you won't steal it." Gas stations are MUCH nicer today than they were in the late 1980's so few people now even know the joy of the old school gas station bathroom or the unmistakably large gas station bathroom keychain. These bathrooms were frequently the actual gates to Hell. That being said, it's probably a good idea that we never got our gas station. We surely would have inadvertently left a door open and accidently unleashed that Hell on the rest of the world. We were just looking for a place to drink beer, not start an Apocalypse.

After college, I wanted to buy an old military Quonset hut to live in. They are big, virtually tornado proof metal buildings that are wide open inside to allow for things like a home roller derby rink or for hiding a giant stolen Frisch's Big Boy statue. My girlfriend at the time actually broke out in a hysterical crying fit because, and I quote, "I DON"T WANT TO END UP LIVING IN A HUT!". I tried to explain that it wasn't like I was looking for her to become a topless Congo woman and live in a grass hut buried deep in a rainforest but she just couldn't grasp the idea of a Quonset hut. Admittedly, even at this later stage of life, I could still totally see myself in a grass hut in the rainforest with a topless Congo woman and endless supply of chocolate milk. Alas, my girlfriend wasn't on board so I had to dump her. I still never got my Quonset hut.

When I finally bought a house, it was sort of disappointing. Sure, it's a great house as far as houses go and I'm truly blessed to have one at all. I just never expected to live in an actual house. I was sure the building I would end up living in would have been an old Fire Department, a Quonset hut, or a giant pyramid made out of laminated taco shells. A traditional house just never really appealed to me. Strangely, traditional houses seem to be what is more commonly available for sale in the world. I have yet to come across a shelter made of laminated taco shells ANYWHERE. And believe me, I have looked.

In an effort to show my wife and children what I perceived to be the "ideal" house, I took them all to Disney World. Pretty much any part of Disney World would make a nice house, in my humble opinion. Walt Disney was a visionary. I don't think he had any actual interest in even living on planet Earth. He pictured himself in a whole other world. And since you could not easily travel to or purchase whole other worlds in the 1950's, he simply began building a whole new world right over the top of this one. I seriously doubt it ever occurred to him that this was an odd thing to do or that it potentially couldn't be done. He just did it.

That's when I realized that home is not just where the heart is, home is where the head is. You can buy a kid the coolest and most expensive toy in the world, and inevitably, they will end up playing with the empty box it came in. Maybe that's why the box always seemed as important to me as the toys in it. I wasn't really a "think outside the box" type of person. I was a "think instead of the box" type of kid. But I ended up with a house...a plain old box.

So I started filling the box with cool toys but that got boring quick. Now I've turned to changing the actual box. Sure it's still just a house, but it's a house with a 1940's theater on it now, and an 18 foot concrete tiki bar out back, and soon six 8 foot tall concrete Moai heads, and eventually a fake mountain with a waterfall and a bar inside it. I can do that..and more...mostly because it never occurred to me that I can't. Thanks Walt.

The point isn't to have an odd house. It's to have a new world. I have three girls and I want their house to be a fantasy and a destination. I want them here as much as I can get them while they grow up. I want their friends here. I want them to see that anything is possible. New worlds can be built over the top of old worlds. I love hearing my daughters say one particular quote...."This is my BEST day ever!". I have been fortunate to hear that a lot. I have to keep raising the bar to keep hearing that. Not just with stuff, but with ideas, conversations, games... and hitting myself over the head with pretty much anything also seems to work for them.

Most importantly, when I'm dead or they are 50 (whichever comes first) and it comes time for them to start dating...I want their main requirement to be finding someone who strives to make each day their "BEST day ever". And just to be sure I'm not missing anything, I start every morning by offering each of my kids a big tall glass of CHOCOLATE milk.

A lecture on why speeches are crazy

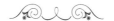

I find my sensibilities are challenged when I hear a crazy street person engaged in a full on solo nonsensical rant. I want to stand close and listen but have a genuine fear that the crazy person will notice me and attempt to turn the rant into a conversation, at which point I will not only lose all interest, but also become uncomfortable. I don't want to participate in someone else's diatribe of lunacy. I just want to be entertained, like watching a movie. I don't think that's too much to ask. If I was wrong about conversation ruining the experience, movie theaters would hire crazy people to sit next to you and say, "Hey, do I look like a squirrel? Buy me a beer." But they don't do that because craziness is NOT an interactive experience. Everyone knows that.

Craziness has long been formally recognized as people talking to themselves, and frequently answering themselves. This act of insanity is also called "giving a speech". If there is any difference in these two things, I am not aware of it. Speech, A.K.A. "crazy-talk", can be easily distinguished from a lecture by its content and target audience.

A lecture usually comes from a source considered in some fashion to be a mentor. It is nothing more than the dissemination of alleged facts from a reliable teacher to a pupil, like when a mother explains to a boy why he should never cook bacon naked.

A speech is generally an unsolicited rambling, intended to express an idea or thoughts, that is forced upon a captive audience or shouted into the faces of people who weren't expecting it at all. It may or may not have an identifiable topic and could be anything from a book report to intimate soliloquy about the night space people probed your rectum with what appeared to be a giant peppermint rowboat paddle.

Ironically, you can be involuntarily committed to a mental facility for crazy-talk or you can get a masters degree in speech. The difference appears to be in whether or not you spout your gibberish on an educational campus or on the street in front of the liquor store. A third option would be to spew forth insanity while wearing a coat and tie and that will land you in a political office and you'll make a ton of money for doing the same thing that you'd have to do for free in the mental institution.

I feel confident in stating these differences because I once intertwined an extended drinking binge with a few years of actual college. The first year of college, I practiced the art of pointless bantering until I felt proficient enough to speak publicly after any kind of alcohol at all, regardless of having purpose or audience. When I learned there was an actual class called "Public Speaking 101" I thought I had found a perfect venue for turning my new skill set into easy credit hours. Boy was I wrong.

I failed my first sober in-class public speaking assignment.... badly.

Much like my prior intoxicated public speaking engagements, I had not actually chosen a topic prior to opening my mouth and thought I would be fine "winging it". Much to my surprise, people were actually listening to me, and expecting some kind of meaning from my words. No one appeared to be drinking or dancing either. This somehow relates to something I once heard about studying under the same conditions in which you will eventually be tested. I was lost. I remember drawing a picture of a giant rabbit on the chalkboard and mumbling a few words about something else before simply returning to my seat and staring at my shoes for a while. I did not receive applause. I also did not receive any of the first four letters of the alphabet on my grade card.

As you might imagine, my instructor kept me after class to give me a LECTURE, not a speech, about why my performance pushed him to the brink of suicide. He even suggested a I get an English translator in case I would be "more comfortable speaking in whatever my native tongue must be". Finally, he whispered to me the one famous traditional and highly bizarre tip that is shared only to those who must speak in public.

"It might help calm your nerves if you picture your entire audience naked."

While I had already heard this same quote from my professor of "Introduction to Serial Sex Crimes" class, it did seem somehow relevant to speech giving too. This concept serves to give you the soothing illusion that you are not actually the most uncomfortable person in the room. The very idea of naked classmates is supposed to take you to a "happy place".

So the next time at the podium I took a moment to imagine my audience, sans clothing, and began my speech with the same line that I use on all my first dates...

"Don't bother running..nobody knows these woods better than me."

Apparently I said a few more things, and the report says that I physically touched a few people in the crowd, but all I remember is failing again and ending up at the municipal hospital for a "mandatory 24 hour evaluation".

The state certified doctor strapped me to a chair and sat down to face me.

"Why don't you start by telling me what you feel inside?", he said.

"Seriously?!?!?", I replied, "I have to give another speech?!?!?! That's what started this whole thing! Do I look crazy to you? Am I nuts? Do I look like a squirrel? Buy me a beer. Then we'll talk."

"Shhhhh!!!", he said, "The movie is starting...."

And that's how I knew the crazy-talk and public speaking were the same thing.

A straight up rant

To sufficiently gauge my level of sophistication, you should know that I was, in fact, just reading an art magazine while perched upon my toilet. I think there is a symbolism there that runs deeper than any words would hope to express. The correlations are endless. Life mimics art.

I'll be honest though, like most of my "reading" endeavors, I like to look at pretty pictures...and should the pictures succeed in confusing my simplistic mind, I will go the extra mile and read the captions. So "reading" might be a strong word. This particular magazine had one picture with a caption that I could not help but notice. The picture was an "abstract" painting and the caption was a quote from the artist that read: "I find my true inspiration when I am reminded to have a heart like a child".

Perplexed, I consulted my Webster's American Pretentious Douche Bag Thesaurus and translated the artist's quote into words I could comprehend. I then verified my finding with the awesome new "BS decoder ring" that was the secret prize in my cereal box this morning. The results were unanimous. What the artist was saying here is that "Any seven year old could have painted this, particularly if they are prone to spasms of the hand, arms, or brain." Interesting.

I personally hate abstract art. I wouldn't eat at a five star restaurant where everything was run through a blender until being rendered completely unrecognizable before being served, but that is what abstract art is to me. I don't want the chef to have to come to my table and declare:

"I wanted to make a simple elegant dish but suddenly I was reminded to have a heart like a child so I just started mashing stuff up with my fingers and then I found this blender thingy that made it all go really fast. It was awesome".

He would say it with a killer French accent of course, but I'd still be angry about it. And then when I got the $200 bill for it, I too would suddenly have the heart of a child and start hitting him with my fists until my mother made me stop it.

I just don't like having to be told what is interesting. If I don't find it interesting on my own, I'm probably not interested in having someone conjure up a ludicrous story to convince me that it is, in fact, totally neat-o. If I see what appears to be the towel that cleaned up the spot where my dog vomited out a box of crayons and you have to explain to me that it's actually intentional art where each layer of new colors symbolizes a new day of your life and how every stroke reinvents the canvas of your being with second chances and hope for tomorrow, I will likely have to stop you and ask this question: "I'm not sure if a human mouth can technically fart, but shouldn't there be some kind of warning before you orally poop?"

Short of politics and first dates, I'm not sure that anything else is marketed with such a staggering amount of nonsensical confabulation. I forgive politicians because politics requires a heavy amount of sleight of hand and mouth to magically redirect it's viewers away from the fact that it has no actual merit in this world, but I hold artists to a higher degree of accountability. No BS is required to sell art, unless what you are selling as art actually isn't art at all. The Mona Lisa required no explanation and was naturally desirable to all who saw it. A single red dot on a large canvas requires a heaping load of bovine dung to explain its importance to the viewer.

I should seize this moment to make a dramatic metaphor about whether your life is a series of beautiful brushstrokes that are inherently desirable to others or a single red dot that requires large doses of BS to pass as interesting, but I'll be honest. I'm just not that deep. Instead, I'm just going focus on that inspirational quote about "having a heart like a child".

It sounds like something a pedophile would say in court. I can even see it being something ordered by a cannibal with a light appetite. But to apply a quote like this to art is almost as ostentatious as... well... using the word ostentatious.

It's one thing to lie. I mean, I've never dated a girl that doesn't think I invented the stringless yo-yo. Where lying crosses the thin line into douchebagism is when you make up the back-story to the lie...like "I invented the stringless yo-yo as a symbolic homage to brave souls on the Underground Railroad, emancipating their brothers and sisters from the similar leash of servitude." Truth be told, there is no "stringless yo-yo". You'd just be throwing a plastic orb on the floor and nothing more would happen. And that could still be fun unless you give people the false expectation that it should mean something more.

I've never been a fan of the song "I believe that children are the future" simply because I can't reward someone for having the keen insight to acknowledge that perhaps children will outlive old people. Someone who would say something so silly is probably the exact same person who interprets art for others.

I don't know why people want to exploit children for the sake of sounding visionary. That's an awful thing to do. Everyone knows you are only supposed to exploit children for cheap factory labor and performing jobs that adult hands are too big to do, like giving breath mints to rattle snakes.

I just thought it was important to take this moment and clarify..every time someone makes up a load of BS to make themselves sound smarter or deeper than they actually are, there is a guy somewhere sitting on the toilet that is going to immediately recognize the excrement that is being spewed forth and call them out on it. Today, I'm that guy.

Q. Who died and made me king?

A. Whomever sold me this porcelain throne with a magazine rack. That's who.

Guest relations

Tonight at work, I gazed up at the television and was pleasantly surprised to see a person that I had punched last year. Because there is no "People I've Punched Network", this is not an experience I get to enjoy every day. The experience was made doubly sweet because I actually punched this particular person AT WORK, which is also something I don't get to enjoy very often.

This heartwarming story began in December of 1989. Like most good fight stories, it began with lots and lots of beer. I don't know what or where I had been drinking but I do know that I managed to find my way to my college dormitory bathroom afterwards. As I entered the common bathroom, I bumped face first into the stomach of a largest white man I had ever seen. It was an irritating occurrence for both of us to have our 3AM progress impeded in either direction. So we did what educated men of that age do. We traded a few punches in the doorway of the bathroom. Thankfully, we were both too inebriated to seriously fight and we kind of exchanged punches in passing and continued on our respective ways without a word being said.

The next day, I was eating lunch in the cafeteria and someone tapped me on the shoulder. I turned around in my seat and immediately recognized the kneecaps I was staring at. It was the giant white man again.

Uh oh.

"Hey man", he said, "Did you throw punches at me last night?"

"Oh yeah", I replied with immediate regret, "and I'm pretty sure you punched me too."

"Do we have a problem?", he asked, "Or are we cool?"

I said, "You look even bigger today so I'm hoping we're cool."

"Good", he said, as he cracked a smile that left my frightened ass slightly less puckered. Then he proceeded to punch me squarely in the chest and walked away.

I responded quickly with words of no known language. I believe what I said was: "Mmmmphhlllaaaa", in a single gasp as all the air exited my body.

The giant white man, it turns out, was the star center of our college basketball team and stood a full seven feet tall and weighed in at around 300 pounds. He was a hard man to miss on campus and, after having him punch me on two separate occasions now, I noticed him pretty much every time he passed by. I, at a paltry 6'1 and 250 was slightly less conspicuous in a crowd. So the next time I saw him walking down the street, I just looked away until we were just getting ready to pass each other. Then I punched him in the belly again...and ran away.

For the remainder of the year, we never said a word to each other, but every time we passed each other we traded a punch or two. It wasn't really fighting, it was just kind of "our thing". They were legitimate punches though and I'm pretty sure it confused the people around us when it happened.

After school ended that year, I never saw him again.

Fast forward twenty years to my latest job. I had just become manager at the restaurant and was enjoying my first week of "Guest relations". The dinner rush was ending and I happened to be walking towards the front door. Suddenly, I saw a giant white man duck under the front door frame. I knew immediately that I recognized this freak of nature. Instinctively, I hid behind the jukebox of the restaurant and waited for the man to pass by. As he did, I jumped out and punched him in the arm.

Immediately the giant white man turned to face me. He appeared angry. I suppose this is a natural reaction to being punched in a restaurant but I hadn't really considered that until seeing his face all red and snarly.

"That's for Ball State", I exclaimed, hoping to diffuse his apparent anger.

"Why Ball State?", he demanded as his hands turned into giant fists of impending punishment.

"Because that's where we got into a fight man", I said, hoping to jar the memory in his large angry head.

"I've never been to Ball State", he replied.

Uh oh.

I immediately realized that I had just made a significant error in judgment...one that might result in serious injury.

I had just punched a really, really large man and apparently I did not know him at all, which might explain why he had a hard time remembering that this was merely "our thing" and not simply the beginning of a very lopsided fight.

"Dude", I said with GENUINE sympathy and fear, "I'm sooo sorry. You look so familiar. I thought I knew you from school."

Just then, one of my employees said, "You DO know him...but from TV. He's on our NBA team."

" Oooooooh yeaaaahhhhh", I thought. THAT'S why he looks familiar. I wonder if he is going to kill me now?

I immediately began thinking of ways to apologize. As manager, it was my job to appease angry guests and turn unpleasant situations into successful new relationships. But even I didn't know the protocol for properly apologizing for jumping out from behind a jukebox and intentionally punching a famous customer. It wasn't like this multimillionaire needed me to buy him a $15 dinner. It turns out that I really wasn't able to make him happy, but more importantly I also never made him mad enough to hit me back. So that's victory enough in my opinion. I can get other customers but these are the only permanent teeth I'll ever have.

I am grateful for one thing. I didn't just punch some random large guy. I punched a bonafide celebrity. Tonight, standing in the bar, looking at a guy on a big screen TV and knowing that I had punched him and lived to tell about it, was a genuinely nice feeling. It felt kind of cool to be able to look at the bartender and say "See that guy right there? Even if you don't believe it, I punched him right here in this restaurant one night."

"You know what's weirder than that?", the bartender replied. "In about an hour, that guy is gonna get out of the shower, put on a suit, and meet his teammates for dinner. They are going to make a few casual suggestions and maybe our restaurant will come up. And then THAT guy is gonna have to tell his team: "Man I don't really wanna go back there. The last time I was there, the manager jumped out from behind the juke box and punched me for no reason at all".

Huh. I never thought about that. What I thought was a pretty good story for me is actually an even better story for him. It's almost like I did him a favor giving him an interesting conversation piece like that. So as a courtesy, the next time a celebrity walks into the restaurant I'm going to jump up and grab the nearest ceiling fan and give them a spinning high kick to the face. You know, for the sake of conversation.

I guess that's why they hired me. I'm gonna put this place on the map.

My favorite conversation from yesterday

Yesterday, after the murder at our motel, I decided to take the kids out for a change of scenery. Because I'm too cheap to actually buy them anything to entertain them, I chose a path that accommodated my desire to be stingy while simultaneously carrying on my family legacy of setting a bad example for my children. Well, legacy might be strong word here for something I'm the first in my family to do but all journeys begin with a single step.

The point is, I drove my kids to the first unplowed parking lot I could find and introduced them to the wonderful automotive experience of "doing donuts". Not much entertains me like seeing my kids faces slammed up against the side windows of the car that's spinning wildly out of control while I yell "WEEEEEEEEEEE!!!!!!!" at the top of my lungs.

No sooner than we began the wintery merry-go-round-of-vomit than my seven-year-old daughter made me as proud as I've even been of any wingman. She, without instruction, screamed out at the top of her young lungs "COP! DADDY COP!!!"

Tears of joy ran down my face. I'm raising a winner. Or a suitable accomplice at the very least.

Her quick thinking saved us a probable fine or impound experience and I quickly realized the error of my judgment. So we drove back BEHIND the Wal-Mart and started over. This time I really got to employ the fine physics lessons I had originally hoped to educate them with and was able to create enough G-forces to render them both completely speechless for several minutes. The silence was mostly from fear, as I assessed from their eyes, but I think the fact that we were pulling nearly seven g's also positioned their little tongues somewhere inside their own left ears might have helped a bit.

When we finally came to a stop. My seven year old gathered her thoughts, wiped the vomit from her chin, and yelled "MORE DONUTS DADDY!" Again, I beamed with pride.

Sadly, at this point my five year old began to cry. But not for the reason I first thought.

"I want a donut", she whispered between tears. "I really do. I want to eat it."

I laughed of course, but that just made her cry more.

"It's not funny!", she yelled, " I'm serious! I'm so hungry. If you drew a picture of a donut, I would eat it. I want one that bad."

Yeah, I feel the same way about donuts. Again, I beamed with pride. However, because I'm cheap, I ended up actually drawing her a picture of a donut, because I could do that for free, and made her eat it, because she had already promised me that she would. Then I went back to making donuts in the Wal-Mart parking lot.

Still, for a few seconds there, I was tremendously proud of both of my children. Parenting is MUCH easier than people say. Look how good I am.

Are we friends?

I like a good fight as much as anybody. I've paid a lot of money to watch particularly bloody battles on television or even in person. I'd even like to see Gladiators brought back. I'd be totally fine seeing the prison system turned into a revenue source instead of a tax burden. Perhaps I'm evil. Violence is by no means the best form of resolution, but it certainly works. It's the reason I'm not British today.

Perhaps my favorite part of fighting though is that it sometimes answers questions that I had not yet even thought to ask. The most important of these questions is "are we friends?". I have a lot of relationships in my life that I've never bothered to define. There are a lot of people that I just "know". However, I always seem to have an immediate answer to the question: "Are we friends?" when I see a person get punched in the face. It's perhaps the best barometer of friendship I know of, and certainly less time consuming than a 50 question survey that compares our common interests.

If I'm eating a delicious cheeseburger and someone walks in the room and smashes their fist into the face of the person I'm eating with, I'm instinctively either going to rise to their defense ask the offender to please pass the ketchup. There is no middle ground. All questions are answered. I'm probably not going to fight for a casual acquaintance. You might deserve what you are getting. I don't know...and I don't wanna break a nail. I'm precious.

There is one form of fighting that blurs even this line though. Couples fights. There are fewer more awkward events than a couples fight. I don't mean two people joining up for a date and going to fight other couples to the death, cause that would actually be pretty cool. I'm talking about when you go out with a couple and they erupt into a fight of their own. It's usually quick, without warning, and totally savage. It conflicts me. I typically consider couples to be one single unit of friendship. When couples fight it's like having a friend with multiple personalities or being attacked by a pregnant bear. You can't punch just one of them because you'll be punching all of them. It boggles my mind. I don't want to hurt the cute little teddy bear in mama's belly but I also don't want to get mauled or have my ears bitten off. Actually, having my ears bitten off might not be that bad. At least then I would haven't to listen to a couples fight again.

The real problem with couples fights is that they are not a spectator sport. Couples want you to "tag-in" and jump in the ring. I paid $100 once to watch Mike Tyson fight Evander Holyfield, but I'm pretty sure I wouldn't have done that if I thought there was a chance that I was going to have to suddenly jump in the ring with either one of them and start fighting too. The ONLY positive outcome of that event is that we do know, for a fact, that Mike Tyson actually will bite off your ear. We already discussed the merits of that.

It's one thing when a friend calls you in the middle of night and asks you to come over with a few gallons of bleach, a used tarp, and a shovel. The fight is obviously already over and you won't have to pick sides. It's another thing entirely when you are sitting at a nice dinner in a public place and two psychotic lovers break out into a verbal duel to the death and one of them says "Can you believe what a jerk YOUR friend is being???" Um....awkward. There is no good answer here.

Worse yet, this couple is probably just going to go home afterwards and have ferocious make-up sex...and you probably won't get the same awkward request to get involved in that. You WANT to answer those questions about who is wrong, but you can't. In the heat of battle, your friends want to hear you say that they are dating the worst person on the planet, but in the morning, when they just got done make-up sexing the same worst person on the planet, they are going to think the you are a jerk for saying bad things about the person they so clearly love. Your friendship doesn't have make-up sex, but it certainly can involve you getting totally screwed on the deal.

It's my opinion, based on years of life experience and the fact that I stayed awake in at least three of my high school psychology classes, is that the only thing you can do during a couples fight is to fight awkward with awkward. As soon as the fight begins, take off your shoes. If the fight continues, take off your shirt. If either party asks for your opinion, you should stand up and take off your pants. This should continue until either the fight stops or until one or all of you is arrested. At least this way, you never picked sides.

There is one other possible solution. When the couples fight begins, and your instincts answer the "are we friends?" question with "No", it's totally game on. Answer all of the fighting couples questions. Make stuff up if you want. Include horrendous and fictitious sexual exploits with tied up farm animals and include Charlie Sheen if you can, just to make it believable. Enjoy the moment. Then afterwards, you can go share this delicious story with someone who really is your friend. That friend will thank you and probably even say something nice back to you, like "Dude, great story. You are truly my friend. I wouldn't let anyone punch you in the face."

Someday I will make the news

One of the biggest pet peeves in my life is seeing or hearing any commercial, for any product, that is presented in the form of a candid conversation between two people. If I'm going to be continually subjected to advertisements for things I will never need, the least they can do is spare me the pretend conversation. I don't need to hear a scripted dialogue between a high school girl and her track coach about how much better her 400 meter hurdle times and general quality of life are since she switched maxi-pads. Save the money, fire the actors, and plagiarize a Visine ad with something simple like "Ernie's Maxi-pads…they get the red out". It's all we really need. There is no award show for best actor in a Maxi pad commercial. It's a single product that needs no introduction or fancy conversation. What is it and what does it do? That's all we care about.

With consideration as to how deeply unsolicited conversation bothers me in commercials, it will probably seem weird to hear that I'm even more bothered by the evening news and newspapers in exactly the OPPOSITE way. The news is not a single topic and generally can't be summarized with a single statement. One topic is okay for a one liner but multiple topics require a legitimate attempt at conversation...like that of a high school girl and her track coach. It needs to "flow", if you'll pardon the pun. You can't just randomly switch topics. There needs to be a segue way of some sort and I'm seriously bothered that strangers in Maxi-pad commercials put more thought into that concept than the people in my own community that deliver my daily news.

I don't want to see a smiling anchorman telling me about the new baby seal pups at the local zoo and then follow up his zany story with a pretend barking seal clap only to turn and face another camera, shuffle his papers, and tell me with a straight face that: "in an unrelated story, half the city just died in a severe gas explosion at the local bean factory."

Seriously, that's not how it should work. I'd never come up to a friend and say "Wow, great new hair cut Johnny! Oh and hey, I just ran over your mom in the driveway. I think she's dead. The good news is that it will be sunny with only a slight chance of rain for her funeral later this week."

I guess I shouldn't expect the news people to treat me in a civilized fashion. They don't even treat each other that way. I can't count the number of times I've seen a horrific news story about some poor kid that died in a silly fraternity stunt and how it depicts the tragedy of "Hazing", only to have the news team immediately cut to a weather report with the "new guy" standing out in subzero temperatures for seven consecutive hours to point out that, indeed, it's cold enough to make your "personal weathervane" look like someone thumb tacked a mouse to your groin. Um...is this NOT hazing?

Seriously, no one needs to actually stand in a snowstorm, or a hurricane, or teetering on the rim of an erupting volcano just to convince me that the weather is indeed exactly what they claim it to be AT THIS VERY MOMENT...in the town where I live...with the exact same weather they are talking about.

You don't need to cut to the shivering newsboy when your studio has windows, made of clear glass, that you could simply point a camera out of to verify your facts. Why risk killing the guy? If you have to send him outside, give him a van. It's like a studio but it's mobile...and guess what? It too has windows! He can talk about the weather from the passenger seat, with the heater on high and a warm cheeseburger in his lap. I WILL believe him. It's not like he's trying to convince me that we put a man on the moon. I won't look at the weather report and say " I just don't know man, that might be one of those vans with the trick windows. Maybe he says it's 90 MPH winds but I don't believe it. I'm not going to let that guy make a fool of me. No sir. Get your ass out of the van and let me see the wind catch your jacket and blow you off the overpass. Then, MAYBE, I'll believe it."

Finally, I'm bothered by the fact that the news claims to present information to me in an "unbiased fashion". That is NOT what I want. I don't choose my friends for their lack of opinions. Share the information with me like a doctor, and then, like a doctor, pretend to empathize with how it might make me feel. Let's bond over this new information. Don't hold back. If a doctor tells me that I've got 12 months to live, odds are he's going to throw me an emotional bone with that bit of news. It can even be something simple, like "I'm sorry brother, dying sucks, but on the plus side, think of all the cool stuff you can buy on "one year same as cash" now! You'll probably never have to pay one dime of that big screen. You'll be gone dude. They can't get money from a dead man and you are looking at maybe 9 months or so of 60" plasma Baywatch babes!....for free! High Five me!"

That's what we call...silver lining. I wish the news would do that. Share an opinion.

If you wanna break the Michael Vick dog fighting story, don't pretend you don't have an opinion. If you want to staple bacon to his face and leave him to fight the dogs, just say it. And then, more importantly, DON'T APOLOGIZE FOR IT LATER. Just once I want to see a newscaster say, "We've been following this story since it first unfolded and I have to tell you, I still don't understand why a no talent tramp "celebrity" is getting more media attention than the fact that your kids won't have a school teacher next year." And then I'd like to see that same newscaster come back the following night, when he is supposed to apologize for his earlier remarks, and simply say "If you want a 'formal retraction' from me, put a bow-tie on my penis and throw me in a cold shower."

That's what I'm looking for. I'd call that guy a friend. I'd watch the news every single night. And if, after two or three weeks, he suggested that I switch maxi-pads, well...hell...I'd probably do it.

Oh yeah, things are gonna be different...someday..when I make the news.

It's getting harder to be stupid

I don't think it's an entirely bad goal to have people look back on your life and say "Wow, that was the longest, most exciting suicide attempt I've ever seen." I'm not saying you need to live every minute "on the edge" but you gotta believe that if you do, the view is always a helluva lot better than it is from the middle. If this weren't true, there wouldn't have to be railings on every balcony in the world. I like to believe that any longevity that I personally incur will be entirely accidental.

I am by no means looking to kill myself at the moment, and even if I said I was, someone would be quick to point out that I bought my Ford Expedition and my Mercury Sable primarily because of their five star crash ratings. The argument could be made that I'm afraid of getting hurt, but an equal argument could be made for the fact that I'm preparing in advance for a spectacular crash.

I do firmly believe that you should taunt death as frequently as possibly, particularly when you are young, because later in life, death is going to start taunting you with stupid things like cholesterol, total body failure, or just sheer old age. You don't want to end a fight like that without having gotten your licks in. Anyone who's ever been in a fight knows the rules:

3. Hit hard

2. Hit a lot.

1. HIT FIRST

I made a LOT of particularly stupid decisions when I was "growing up", and I have to say that, in retrospect, I'm exceedingly pleased that I did. Sure, some were embarrassing or hurtful, and certainly none were well-thought out, but for the most part, none left any unacceptable permanent damage that anyone can prove. Some of my greatest memories should well have been my last actions on Earth. The only reason I bring this up is because, well...frankly...I miss it.

There are conflicting philosophies on whether "wisdom comes with age" or that "age comes only from wisdom". I personally don't believe I've lived this long because I'm smart. Squirrels have been running out in front of cars for close to 100 years and there is still no shortage of squirrels. If you ask the people in cars, they will say "the squirrels are driving me nuts", and if you ask the squirrels, they will say "the nuts are driving me". Like most squirrels, my nuts have likely been driving me most of the time. Damn the traffic. I'm on a mission.

I guess that is what sucks about not dying. After a while, it sort of becomes an unconscious habit.

I find this "wisdom" thing to really be cramping my style. I'm not as eager to try things that hurt now. And as for the "age" thing, I don't heal as fast as I used to. I think people watch fewer cartoons as they get older NOT because they are less interesting, but more because we are not looking to them as often for inspiration for new things to try. After a long series of trials and errors I have become more and more convinced that I will never randomly fly on my own...more than once...thus eliminating the desire to try jumping off a ledge again.

I miss that about my youth. God gave me parents so that someone would be scared for me when I was too stupid to be scared for myself. Now, I've gone and had kids of my own. And as luck would have it, I love them dearly. Now it's getting harder and harder to be stupid. I still want to try the stuff I've seen on cartoons, but I end up doing more of the stuff I see on Hanna Montana than I do of the stuff I see on Family Guy. Not that I don't want to battle Norm McDonald as the Grim Reaper, it's just not as practical as it used to be. And that saddens me.

Sure, I still buy amusement parks, movie theaters, diners, bowling alleys, and old cars each week but it's a poor substitute for the unspeakable abuses of the past. I'm still out on the balcony but these days I find myself just sitting in a chair, checking out the view, and knocking back a tasty margarita. It's not all bad, but sometimes after a few drinks, I still kind of think that maybe I really can fly.

Passing Time

When I drive a car, I speed. I break the law 100% of the time. I don't speed because I'm late. I speed because it's fun and because life is short. If I can save 15 minutes a day heading to work for 20 trips a months, that gives me 60 extra hours a year to waste on something else...like Facebook or EBay. That's almost three whole days I get free, just for speeding a little bit every day. Awesome.

However, when I speed, I consider myself to be quite courteous about it. I'm sober, I use my turn signals, I give right of way, I let people merge in front of me, I wave when they reciprocate, I don't tailgate, and I rarely get airborne. I try not to attract attention to myself. I like the time in my car and use it wisely. I chair dance, pick my nose, sing loudly and off key, and all of the other things that folks enjoy while driving a car at twice the legal limit. Driving is fun.

So when someone else interrupts my fun, I get very, very annoyed. I don't enjoy being tailgated. I hate it when people cut me off to try to merge at the last possible second, and above all else, I really hate it when people who are driving slowly just cannot accept being passed. If I live a thousand years, God forbid, I will never understand this particular traffic phenomenon.

Men in large trucks seem to be the most guilty of the non-pass-ables. I can be driving along at 90MPH minding my own business and see a pickup truck in the slow lane way up ahead driving maybe 60MPH. I close the gap immediately and just as I signal to pass, the guy in the truck stomps the gas and decides that we are racing. His very ego is at stake. Life will end if I pass him.

Personally, I don't care if he wants to drive faster than me. Actually I prefer it. He can distract the cops for me. And I won't ever have to pass him, which is great, because....well, I don't care. If he wants to go fast, then by all means, go fast. If he wants to go fast because I'm doing it, I'm flattered. But please, he should continue going fast until he is well out of my way. At a constant speed, I should NEVER pass anyone more than once. It's a crime that should be punishable by death. But it happens to me literally every day.

It happened again tonight as I was travelling down a four lane state road. I passed a Jeep Cherokee like it was parked. Up ahead the road merged down to one lane in each direction and I was going to have no one in front of me for miles. Sweet joy of driving! Just as I passed through the final stoplight, I saw the Jeep in my rear view mirror, giving it all the gas it had, and flying back up on me. He was really going to be cutting it close to pass me before the road merged but it was obvious he was going to try. Annoyed but still without enough sponsorship to race him, I decided I would let him pass. Conceding to his amazing desire to overcome his small penis would not cost me much time and I simply didn't care to challenge him. However, just as he was passing me, I saw some-thing...just barely...out of the corner of my right eye. A shadow maybe.

I had the terrible feeling, like when you are boating and round the corner of a stream to find that you are at the top of a giant waterfall. The shadow that I saw was huge, and it was moving fast. It was big, like a brontosaurus, but fast like high school relationship. I wasn't sure it was even real as it passed in front of me. But as the Jeep that was running parallel to me on my left exploded into pieces on impact, I realized the shadow WAS real.

It was a deer. Not just any deer. A buck. And not just any buck. It was the father of all land mammals. The Arnold Schwarzenegger of the deer world. The supreme animal sacrifice gifted to me from the driving Gods as penance to the Jeep driver for being such a tremendous douche bag. Ideally, this is how all such traffic incidences should conclude. Total carnage. The Jeep was obliterated and the driver never hit the brakes. Even after the contact, he sped off into the darkness with no functional headlights and large portions of his vehicle scattered in his wake. Too embarrassed to stop I suspect.

I immediately thanked the car gods, not only for letting me witness the karmic joy of the event, but also for letting me remain calm enough not to speed up. If I had, it would have been me who hit the deer.

My joy was immediately tempered by the fact that an animal had just been hit by a four thousand pound projectile piercing through the darkness at 75MPH. I like animals way more than I like people, so this bothered me. If I had been racing a deer and the deer had run over a Jeep, I would have continued driving with no qualms at all. But an animal was down, and I had to check on it. I'm weak like that.

I slowed down and finally got turned around to head back for the deer. I drove through a few thousand dollars of Jeep parts very slowly looking for signs of the deceased or maimed animal. I saw nothing. The point of impact was obvious. Most of the Jeep was still there. But there was no buck.

It was then that it occurred to me..."what the hell would I do if I DID find an injured deer?" It's not like I'm going to pick up a pissed off 500 pound horned animal and stuff it into my car for a ride to the vet. It was waaaay to big to simply drive over a few times to ensure it was dead like I do with injured humans. And the only other option I had was to mercy kill it in some other manner. With the car itself ruled out, my remaining choices were to get out and tackle the deer and choke it with my bare hands until it quit breathing, while whispering slowly in its ear "Just let it happen Mr. Buck...let it happen" or to open the trunk of my car and get the only weapon I had on me...a Chinese AK-47 assault rifle. I can't really see my standing on the side of major state road, near an open gas station and firing off short bursts of semi-automatic rifle fire into the darkness and not attracting some kind of Federal attention that I didn't want.

Finally, I came to accept that maybe the deer was just fine. I did see it run off after the impact. He was probably at a Deer bar somewhere telling his buddies how he just totally wasted some jackass in a JEEP. I like to think so anyway. By this point I was so wound up and ready for a mercy kill, that I just got back into my car and went looking for the guy in the Jeep.

I never found him either. I guess it was a good day. I didn't even have to use my AK.

2OOMPH

I was a kid when cars first passed the 200MPH mark at the Indianapolis 500 Mile Race. I recall hearing Mario Andretti discuss this milestone by saying, "Honestly, 200MPH doesn't really feel that fast when you are racing. It's when you are spinning backwards towards a concrete wall that you realize just how fast it is". I think that's a great race quote, but it took me nearly 30 more years to realize that it's a much better quote about getting older.

2011 is the year that, should I continue my 39 year annual trend of not dying, should deliver unto me my 40th birthday. That's a funny number because it's completely inconceivable to my 5 and 7 year old daughters and totally enviable to my 76 year old father. To me, it's just kind of weird.

Those who know me, know that I'm monumentally nostalgic. I embrace the past, even though I've forgotten a great deal of it already. I've even become a passionate purveyor and sometimes collector of antiques, which grows increasingly funny each year as I become one myself. It's kind of like a bird sneaking onto an airplane.

There was a time when I distinctly remember wishing I was 16, then 18, and finally praying for the day of my 21st birthday. I remember thinking my 22nd birthday was handy in case i became totally dyslexic. But after that, I was looking through the genie manual for the rewind button the magic lamp. Wishing you were older is perhaps the dumbest thing you can ever wish for. To quote my friend Sara Wiley: "It's a bell you just can't unring".

In that 200MPH sprint from 16 to 39, I've gone from checking out hot 16 year-old girls to wondering what father would ever let their girl leave the house looking like that. However, I do still totally check out the under dressed 18 year-old hottie though because I'm just pushing 40, not dead.

Even then, I can't relate to an 18 year-old on ANY level. This is someone who doesn't know the joy of an old blues record on scratched up vinyl. Hell, they wouldn't even know what a vinyl record was. I have three 18 year-old girls in my employ that don't know how to read "a clock with hands". Seriously. It's all digital baby.

These kids never knew what it was not to have a "people mover" at the airport. I remember running with 20 suitcases hanging off every available digit to catch the last flight to spring break. It was a rat race. Now I'm on that people mover with no particular destination but the ground beneath my feet is carrying me there faster than I need to arrive. And dammit, when I get there, they are probably going to strip search my wrinkled up gelatinous body in front of the perfectly toned teenagers just to make sure I'm not out to blow them all up. Sure, I'm jealous, but I am not a terrorist.

So here I am, facing another New Years Eve...2011.

I will turn 40. I will have been married for TEN years. I will have two kids that know more about my computer than I do and another that still thinks I'm just a furry lump that brings food sometimes and makes the poop go away. And in what will seem like 15 more minutes, I'll be saying the same thing about turning 50, being married for 20 years, and wondering if my two kids know that the checks I'm going to write for college are totally going to bounce and the third kid will wonder why I'm not as furry anymore, can barely chew my own food, and sometimes poop myself.

200MPH didn't seem that fast when I was racing but now that I'm spinning backwards, that concrete wall is looking pretty vicious.

"Mario is slowing down in the back stretch".

Oh well... Happy New Year.

Do not consume raw cookie dough?

Few people have ever gone to church, listened to a sermon, and NOT felt like they were being singled out and spoken specifically to. It's happened to me. I've certainly provided MANY opportunities to myself to feel that particular guilt.

On the bright side is that, outside of a church, I pretty much never listen to anything and generally consider myself exempt from all rules and regulations. For example, I speed everywhere I go...and not just a little. It's not because I'm in a hurry, but because it's so darn fun to go fast. If I get a ticket, it's not punishment, it's a joy tax, and they use the money to build new roads that I can go even faster on. It's a win/ win.

This week, I've been temporarily stricken with a variety of odd ailments that required the visiting of a doctor and the use of medications. I felt genuinely bad for the nurse as I watched her type up all of this warning and instructional mumbo jumbo and then felt equally bad for the pharmacists as they attempted to explain the drugs, effects and side effects, while I blankly stared through them and into the candy rack behind them and made sweet love in my own head to stack of delicious chocolate truffles as their packaging seemed to dance in the soft light of the pharmacy fluorescents...

But I managed to secure the marvels of medical salvation and the accompanying instructions and take them to the cashier where I also purchased a much needed package of Nestle's Tollhouse "Break and Bake" Chocolate Chunk Lovers cookies.

When I got home, I immediately ripped open the cookies because, despite not reading the directions for the medication, I was positive that I should be taking them with food. What better than cookies?

I had no intention of baking them of course. I'm not sure if the oven here even works. Eating baked cookies is like adopting an adult cat. You've already missed the best part.

The only real question in my mind is "what kind of beer goes best with cookies AND antibiotics? They don't teach you those things at wine tastings or at the pharmacy. And that's when it happened...

Out of the corner of my eye, on a small piece of paper attached to the bag that contained my antibiotics was a word I instantly recognized....

ALCOHOL.

Yep, right there, on the medicine bag itself. It was like church all over again. God was speaking directly to me! Singling me out in my time of need. I can't articulate my sadness in words when I took the chance to read further...it was not a recommendation for beer pairing at all. It was a ....a...a ...warning.

Wow. That sucked. It was a lot like opening the biggest Christmas present under the tree. One you'd been eyeballing for weeks. Anticipating the live pony that surely awaited you inside the box. Only, when you opened the box, there really was a pony...but it was dead... and there was a note attached to it saying that the pony needed to be fed every 24 hours or it would die. And it was your fault because you left the pony in a box, under the tree, for weeks, imagining it would be even more awesome if you waited until the day you were SUPPOSED to open it.

This is what directions mean to me: Dead ponies. I hate directions.

And yet, I had read them. The information was in my head now. And I hated it.

NO ALCOHOL with medication. Seriously?!?!?

I took a bite of my deliciously chunky chocately cookie dough and wondered aloud...what could be worse than this?

And then I saw the wrapper from the cookie dough and noticed the HUGE warning on both sides of the package..."DO NOT CONSUME RAW COOKIE DOUGH".

I nearly cut out my own eyes with a spoon just so the words would stop haunting me. But instead of cutting out my own eyes, I hoisted that spoon and used it to dig up the most magnificent ball of raw cookie dough ever to be lifted in a single glob and I shoveled it into my giant fat face and chased it with a delicious Samuel Adams beer...and some medicine.

There is probably going to come a day, and sooner rather than later, when I'm going to wake up one last time in a hospital bed, with my pastor hovering over me, muttering some mumbo jumbo about "last rights" and I know ....I'm going to have that same eerie feeling that that he is just singling me out again.....

But in case anyone is wondering, THIS IS WHY MEN DON"T STOP AND ASK FOR DIRECTIONS. Dead ponies I tell you. DEAD PONIES!!!!

I hate technology

I tried to post a piece of one of my books tonight on the internet and found out an interesting fact about myself. I'm not smart enough to make it happen. I tried the old "cut and paste" method that I normally use, but apparently that method is only good for making ransom notes now, if hypothetically, I did that sort of thing. I can't copy the story but I also I can't help but think there is some kind of cosmic intervention happening here. It's almost as if a higher power is wagging a tisk-tisk finger at me and inviting me to rethink the occasion. Sure, the story involved violence, a few law infractions, one or two actual felonies, two homeless people, Jesus, lots of alcohol, and smidgen of jail time... but overall, I felt like it had a happy ending. You know, something the kids could really be proud of.

The truth is that I hate technology and technology hates me right back. I collect cars and Americana from the 1930' to the 1950's because the world made sense back then. These days, there is all this stuff, like Facebook, that isn't really NEEDED but is supposed to make our lives better. It's true I guess. I have like 700 "friends" here I haven't seen in years. That's livin' the good life right? And I for some reason feel the need to share tales of woe and debauchery here? There's an old saying "Just because you can, doesn't mean you should".

Case in point... I have a cell phone, which I totally hate. I remember the good old days when I'd leave my house and no one could find me. Other than the time I was abducted and used as a guinea pig for cross breeding humans with plants, that kind of inaccessibility was generally a good thing. Fortunately, my cell phone sucks. I can't even get a signal in my own house. Granted that might have something to do with the fact that I coated the entire outside of my home with tin foil to keep the aliens from reading my thoughts, but still...I think some of the blame has to go to AT&T for not addressing that particular concern with their customers. I'm surely not the only one who believes...

My phone is capable of doing more things than the computer that controlled the Apollo missions to the moon. It's got games, e-mail, internet, music, alarms, calendars, a camera, video, a calculator, a fax machine, a printer, a coffee maker, and the ability to designate ring tones to sound like Mariah Carey farting. It's impressive...I'm told....but not to me because, even worse than not knowing how to use the stupid thing is the fact that, I don't know how to UNUSE it.

Seriously, I can't intentionally whip out my phone and access the internet. My phone has the ability. I don't. I can't even type in an internet address anyway, because my giant sausage-like fingers hit whole rows of keys on that inexplicably tiny keyboard. So when I started getting phone bills of excessive internet use, I became instantly suspicious. I do not use the internet on my phone. My pants, however, apparently spend quite a bit of time on the internet. Every time I pull this evil device from my pocket, I see that my pockets have managed to unlock all of the technological secrets that my brain cannot comprehend. My pants can find the breeding habits of the North American penguin on the internet and I couldn't successfully dial 9-1-1 on a bet. That's pretty crappy. Seriously, my phone has taken more pictures inside my pants than Brett Favre's phone. Certainly not on purpose. I shudder to think who my pants have chosen to e-mail these pictures to. But if you did get them, and you like what you see...call me...

I'm a Leo.

I once watched the Fox Network in Spanish for a month because my five year old changed some kind of setting with the remote control that I was never able to figure out. I finally solved the problem... by selling the house. I'm not even joking. I have no idea how stuff like that happens but I can't make it UNHAPPEN. There's another old saying "the main difference between a pregnant woman and light bulb is that you can unscrew a light bulb." I don't know who originally said that but it's probably the same bastard that invented the Rubik's Cube and my cell phone.

So I'm not posting any stories tonight. Maybe tomorrow my ass will text it to you, along with a picture of itself. I don't know. What I do know is that I'm looking for a nice rotary cell phone and kind of missing my old etch-a-sketch. If you are one of the six people that takes the time to read my long and pointless diatribes/notes I apologize for the absence thereof. Maybe someday some fool will publish my books and you can read them in the bathroom, the way God intended.

I need a Holiday

I was having beers with a friend of mine who is either British, Australian, or just talks with a cool accent to sound like Mad Max or Crocodile Dundee in hopes of picking up chicks. I really should ask him at some point what causes his funny talk, but I guess I've always assumed it was just the beer. He might well be British though, so I'm going with that option for the sake of this conversation.

I was expressing to my friend that I've lately began experiencing some anxiety over what I should do when I grow up. Given that, statistically speaking, I'm more than half dead already, it seems like now is maybe the last chance to figure this all out. When you are facing 40 and looking down the hall at death, you can't dilly dally with any more time wasting... and we all know that there is no greater oracle for seeing a clear path to the future than to stare down a full glass of Guinness draught with Mad Max.

He sat quietly and listened to my tale of woe and drank numerous beers on my dime before offering a single piece of advice to me.

"Mate", he said, "You need a Holiday".

As usual, because of that damned accent, and perhaps because my bloodstream was flammable at this point in the evening, I had no idea what he was talking about. It seemed to be two different things. Mate? Holiday? I already have three kids, so I feel fairly confident that I've got that whole "mate" thing down pat. "Holiday", on the other hand.....hmmm...

I'm not entirely sure how one goes about getting a Holiday. I've always thought that was like a nickname or a venereal disease...in that it's something you can't give to yourself. Admittedly, it would be REALLY cool to have a Holiday. I'm not out to compete with Christmas or anything but something subtle, like St. Patrick's Day sounds pretty nice.

I am not sure that I've done anything special enough to deserve a Holiday of my own though. I've certainly not driven the snakes out of Ireland, but I have driven some Irish people home from bars.

Have I ever been resurrected from the dead like Jesus? Well, yes actually. My resurrection required a few doctor's and some stomach pumping but still...it DID happen on a Holiday. Groundhog's Day actually, one thousand-nine-hundred-and-ninety-two years after Jesus did it, so it hardly garnered similar attention. Plus, there was that whole thing about him doing it so save the rest of the world part, whereas I just was drunk.

That got me thinking...if a freakin Groundhog can get a holiday... maybe it's not so farfetched for me to get one...

What, precisely, did this rodent do to deserve his own Holiday? He climbed out of a hole and checked to see if he had a shadow. Wow. Real cool there Mr. Rodent. That certainly deserves a Holiday. I'm sure Jesus was looking at February 2nd on his calendar and thinking to himself: "Geez, THAT'S all I had to do???" I think not.

I'm betting even the Groundhog is confused by the media attention he gets every year. For him, it's kind of like getting up in the morning to check the obituary, just to make sure he isn't in it. "Do I have a shadow today? Cool. I'm good. Who wants whiskey?"

The groundhog is likely clueless that an entire country uses this event to determine whether or not winter is over. As a people, humans are pretty stupid. The groundhog is technically a land beaver. A furry little rodent. If you are standing out in the cold, looking for a beaver....well, I've got lots of jokes for you....but rather than checking the rodent for a shadow, a smart man would kill him and make a hat. If a rodent doesn't have a shadow, he's either a vampire or it's dark out. Get a clue. But I'm not here to judge, I'm here to get a Holiday.

As far as Holidays go, I've always felt like Canadian Boxing Day was perhaps the dumbest one....once I found out that there was no actual fighting involved. Then again, I'm not a huge fan of Canadians. Nothing personal, I just hate what they've done to bacon. Plus, you know, they speak French in North America. Honestly, who does that? I'm a little ashamed to share the continental name of "North America" with them. They should be "Northier Americans" if they speak English or "Eastern France" if they don't. I'm not trying to be a xenophobe here, I'm just SERIOUSLY pissed about the bacon thing. In America, we already discovered Ham. It's not new. But those French speaking bastards had to go off and act all nationalistic..."Oh Non Messieurs...c'est Bacon! Canadienne Bacon!" Well, it's not. It's Ham. So take your stupid Boxing Day and kiss my ass. But don't "French" kiss it...damn Canadians...

Anyway, back to me.

I guess I really don't even need my "own" Holiday per se. I'd settle for sharing a Holiday. I'm not greedy. I think a lot of Holidays would be more fun if they were merged with other Holidays anyway. Take "Grandparents Day" for example: Imagine for a minute, a perfect world, where Canadian Boxing Day didn't suck, and was actually about fighting. Then combine these things for "Grandparent Boxing Day". How awesome would that be?

Combine Valentines Day with Halloween and you've got yourself the role playing date of the year. If an adult chick dressed up as a hot nurse rings my doorbell in Mid-February looking for candy from a stranger, she came to the right place! Actually, that's how I met my wife and that would be totally less weird if it had been part of a Holiday or something. Let's make this happen!

So I've got this narrowed down now, at least in my head, that I do want a Holiday but I don't want the pressure of it being mine exclusively. Given that I am actually a huge fan of land beaver, I choose to tap into Groundhog's Day. Neither of us are totally deserving of our own day but we could totally be calendar roommates. We can call it "NoHogginThe Day". It's going to be awesome but I have no idea what it's going to mean but I'm pretty sure there's going to be beer involved. You don't have a shadow when you're passed out on the floor. Maybe you stupid humans can do something with that.

Yeah...it's gonna be a loooong winter.

Howard Hughes and the key to celebrity

These days, most people have had the privilege of sleeping in an adjustable bed, either through a chance encounter with a hooker half their age at a seedy fantasy themed motel, or simply because of an extended hospital stay dealing with horrific injuries obtained while trying to replicate actions seen on cartoons. What most kids today don't realize, is that they can thank a celebrity for the wonderful experience of lying in an adjustable bed. The first fully adjustable bed was conceived and commissioned by famous engineer, aviator, and rich guy, Howard Hughes. Full time genius and part time freak, Howard Hughes pioneered this fantastic machine, making life easier for future hospital patients all over the world and making kinky sex possible again for all the worlds elderly who can no longer get their legs over their own heads by use of their own muscles. If you don't have a mechanical bull, the adjustable bed is quite possibly the greatest mechanical creation of our time.

In case you were wondering if celebrities and super freaky rich guys have already addressed all of our needs and creature comforts, the answer is a resounding NO. Mr. Hughes created the adjustable bed while lying in a hospital bed, close to death, after a plane crash. He was simply not comfortable lying flat on his back. This point of conception was not lost on me tonight as I sat, rather uncomfortably, on the toilet across the hall from my home office.

"Man", I thought to myself, "This toilet sure would be nicer with a reclining backrest and a nice footrest". While nothing could be immediately done to satisfy my urge to lean further back on the toilet, I did spy an opportunity to elevate my feet while I was working other things out. Strangely enough, my sporty new footrest was nothing more than a regular magazine rack that had apparently been in the bathroom, serving lesser purpose, for some time now. I found it odd that there would even be a magazine rack in our bathroom since I don't read and my wife, like all women, doesn't poop.

With my sudden new awareness of the world and a new focus on the magazine rack, I really had time to appreciate my surroundings and bask in my new accomplishment. My curiosity of the magazine rack quickly grew. What was thing even doing in my bathroom? What was in it?

The answer...ironically, was that, in addition to a few requisite car magazines, the rack contained, and actually featured, my wife's collection of celebrity gossip magazines. Smut, as I call it. Still, I was embraced by a philosophical circle of life...beginning with a crippled celebrity with his feet propped up in a hospital and feverishly making notes, and ending with me, temporarily crippled with my feet propped up beside the toilet and feverishly reading celebrity notes. The bond was timeless and transcended mere social or economic class.

Feeling as if old Howard himself was whispering inspiration into my ear, I quickly leafed through the celebrity gossip magazine hoping to glean more inventive "gold" from celebrities that I could translate to a better bathroom experience. What I found was... pictures! I LOVE PICTURES! I certainly would never have waited months to open this magazine if I had any possible way of knowing that I would not actually have to READ anything! This was fantastic!

My enthusiasm was quickly quashed by reality. The first four full pages of the magazine and it's glossy pictures were devoted solely to convincing the subscriber that celebrities are, and I quote "JUST LIKE US". As if proof of such a thing were required, the four page spread depicted famous people performing completely mundane tasks like: shopping, driving a car, eating a cheeseburger, walking a dog, or accidentally exposing some ass fat on the beach. Awesome... just like the average Joe would do it. As if we had no idea that celebrities still had to eat food.

I was dumbfounded that people actually spend money to buy magazines showing other human beings doing the same boring things that the people buying the magazine do every day also. Had I known that content was completely irrelevant, I would have actually started a magazine a long time ago and not wasted ten years doing market studies on whether or not people would actually accept my strange love of goats and my need to photograph them wearing various aerosol based food products. I had been over thinking this all along.

Still, I felt like the magazine was wrongly portraying the similarities between celebrities and regular people. Instead of glossy pictures that tout..."LOOK! Celebrities are just like you...except way prettier and with a whole lot more money!", the magazines should have been saying, "Dude, look, except for your crappy job, you could totally be a celebrity yourself!".

I think Howard Hughes would be pretty upset to see me sitting on a toilet looking at pictures of Barry Manilow walking his Chihuahua on the beach, when clearly I should be designing a reclining toilet, maybe even with a cup holder. He'd be angry that I idly watched some young famous girl snort cocaine off a golden framed mirror with a rolled up $100 bill when I should be inventing an automated inhaler that could dispense the drug on a time released program that would allow her to keep both hands free to do...well...whatever the hell it is that she does to be famous. Anyway, you get the point.

Celebrities generally do SOMETHING. People reading about celebrities generally don't do anything. I'm no rocket scientist but I suspect that MIGHT be the real difference between them...or at least that was the way it used to be..

Perhaps too, wealth comes from doing SOMETHING as opposed to just reading about other people doing something and then buying pictures of those people even when they actually aren't doing anything.

That's just something to think about the next time your legs go numb while sitting on toilet for 20 minutes with no footrest. Seize the day, invent the future, do SOMETHING. Ask yourself, "How would Howard Hughes poop?" And then go make the world a better place. You can still die alone and crack-whore crazy, but if you leave a legacy and have big money, it's eccentric and NOT crazy. That, my friends, is the key to celebrity.

Unfinished business

I recall reading an interview of Kevin Bacon in GQ Magazine many years ago. I had to read it because, as many of you are aware, Kevin and I know lots of the same people...every seventh one as I understand. In the conversation, the subject of Kevin's sexual conquests came up. Apparently there have been quite a few. When you are named after meat, that kind of thing is going to happen I suppose.

Specifically, Kevin mentioned the first time that he realized, as a man, he had "game". He said that as a celebrity, you can hook up with anyone at any given time. It requires no skill at all. Before Kevin was a celebrity, he was a mere restaurant waiter. As a waiter,

Kevin covered more ladies than Victoria Secret did. That is no small achievement.

While I am in no way comparing myself to Kevin Bacon, I am totally envious of..his being named after meat. My name is a bit boring. I'm pretty sure my collegiate escapades would have been substantially more exciting if I would have walked into a party and everyone screamed "Ron Sausage is here!" It just sends a message.

Anyway, the important thing I realized from the Kevin Bacon interview is that every man needs to be in touch with his Mojo. Kevin was in touch. He was a gamer and he knew it. A lot of men struggle to ever have that validation. That hurts a fellow. You need confidence in this world.

So I was "talking" on Facebook to my friend Ericka today and somehow we stumbled onto the topic of principles. Odd, since I'm not renowned for being highly principled. I did, however, remember a story involving my grade school PrinciPAL. That story led me to realize that I have "unfinished business". Hence, this story.

In grade school, I was not yet concerned with whether or not I "had game". I didn't even know what "game" was yet. What I did know is that I was really, really good at peeing. Better than most kids, I suspected. As fortune would have it, there came a time when I was able to display my special skills to my classmates. Sadly, this could not happen IN the classroom, so off to the little boys room we marched.

I lined up at the urinal...the short one...not the tall one...I was already comprehending the subject of trajectory... AND I was like three feet tall. I began to let loose a gentle stream that made a glistening golden rainbow that arched from my little body directly over to the porcelain wall mounted urinal. With skillful precision, I began to back up. Step by little step, the golden rainbow arched higher and farther. Frankly, it was beautiful and I was a little disappointed not to see a tiny leprechaun leap into the urinal as it happened. I continued backing up until I actually entered the handicapped stall behind me. To anyone entering the bathroom at this time, it would simply appear that the handicapped stall itself was peeing across the aisle and into the urinal. Probably a freaky thing to see.

Sadly, the principal of Acton Elementary did NOT see the rainbow. He did however walk directly through it. I put a nice warm horizontal racing stripe directly across the left leg of my principals dress trousers. This, my friends, is how a little pee goes from simply great to LEGENDARY. I peed on THE BOSS...something I've wanted to do many times since then in my life but never again accomplished.

I remember being "paddled" relentlessly for that one but no amount of paddling would trump my peeing on him. I won. I'm sure that guy remembers me. I'm ashamed that I don't remember his name.

Not too many years later, I was in my front yard playing "hide and go seek" when it occurred to me that I needed to pee again. Well, that makes it sound like I had waited several years to pee again...I didn't. That was just a segue way.

Anyway, I was hiding in the bushes in my front yard and I needed to pee. Not willing to give up my awesome hiding spot, I decided to pee in the bushes. Like any kid riddled with attention deficit disorder, I immediately began to wonder if my legendary golden arch could make it out of the bushes, across the sidewalk, and into the actual yard. As luck would have it, I did possess that particular skill set.

The other kids were still looking for me, including my buddy's totally hot sister. As she came running around the front of the house, she never saw me. For reasons I cannot fathom, she never thought to stop and check whether or not the bushes had their own magical stream of urine emanating from them for no apparent reason. Accordingly, "hot sister" became the second person to get pinstriped my golden stream of greatness.

Once again, paddling ensued...this time by my father. A correlation was made in my head that day and out my sheer desire to make people stop beating my ass, I elected to never pee on anyone again.

Fast forward about ten years and I got a date with my buddy's hot sister. This was the exact moment in my life when I realized that I had "game". I peed on a girl and then got a date with her. I marked the territory. I owned the territory. I ruled. My award was a lifetime of confidence.

Today, in "talking" to Ericka, I realized the glitch in my game. I have "unfinished business". My game is incomplete. Many guys have a list in their head that they need to cross off: blondes, brunettes, red headed hotties, the double jointed Asian girl, identical twin dwarf chicks, whatever...before they can "settle down".

Personally, I thought I was done with all that. Until today. I have a blotch on my record. I know it now. I've only dated HALF of the people I've peed on. I'll admit it, that shakes my confidence a little bit.

I'm not gay very often, and there is a strong chance my grade school principal is dead now, but in spite of those trivial details, I kind of feel like that guy owes me a date.

I tried explaining that to Ericka and it only made it more clear in my mind. She simply responded with "Well, you ARE from Acton". That's why we are friends. Some people get all weird when I confess my need for gay necromancy with people I've peed on. She doesn't.

I just hope my wife understands.

I know Kevin Bacon does.

A casual birthday reflection... since no one wants a formal birthday reflection that would require my birthday suit again.

As the tractor beam of cruelty pulls me towards another allegedly "landmark" birthday, I'm forced to consider my fleeting mortality and the legacy/mess I'll leave behind after my impending demise. Dying isn't so much a fact of life so much as life is necessary precipitation of death. Life is plausible without death but death is pretty darned dependent on life. That being recognized, I'm looking into the possibility of simply not dying. On the outside chance that plan fails to reach fruition, I thought it best to post my thoughts on the remaining days I have.

The meaning of life is a snowflake. It's a million very temporary interpretations on one thing and all eventually melt away to make room for new flakes. Mortality is a cruel joke that impedes our ability to be relevant to future generations of flakes, despite our overwhelming desire to do so. Life is generally perceived as that temporary accumulation of time, experience, and wisdom of one flake, and that flakes fanatical quest to pass along that experience to whole new generation of flakes who don't particularly care. It's an uphill battle to be sure, and rarely do snowflakes roll uphill. I'm increasingly aware of that, as with each passing birthday I feel the sun beat down a little warmer on my fluffy white skin.

Honestly, I don't feel old yet...most of the time. Maybe that's because I was wise enough to steal all of the mirrors in my home from a travelling carnival seven years ago. The carnival mirrors lull me into a false sense of being where I've grown quite comfortable. I have different rooms in my house where I can feel as tall or as skinny as I need to feel that day. Although some say it's best to occasionally see yourself through other people's eyes, I've always personally felt that it seemed a little gross to rip off someone else's face and use it as a mask just so that you can look at yourself. Maybe I took that too literally but I don't want to risk the murder charges just yet.

As I pontificate the legacy I'm leaving for my three baby girls, I realize that I'm likely doomed to the same relegation of fate that I perceived my parents and grandparents to exist in. My kids are likely going to fancy themselves to be too young and hip to derive any real-value life counsel from their ear-shaving, gray-haired, bed-wetting, shell of a man, who is more renowned for telling them to wear longer shorts than for being the vast pool of wisdom and knowledge that I fancy myself to be. That unbridgeable gap in perception is made even more blatant by the fact that I used the phrase "I fancy myself", while no self-respecting kid would ever dare utter those words. But dammit, I AM fancy...right down to my fancy pants. And I DID learn a thing or two along the way...

Or did I?....

Rita Mae Brown said "Good judgment comes from experience, and often experience comes from bad judgment." While that is certainly an entertaining quote to read, I don't know that I completely subscribe to its truth. I've learned, over these many years, that I am completely and wholly capable of taking a bad experience, that was born of woefully bad judgment, and using it as a tool to learn absolutely nothing. Further, I have gone on to repeat similar, exact, or even greater errors in judgment later in this same life...each time with astonishingly and similarly bad results. Thus I have proven experience to be completely independent of actual wisdom.

Much as I earlier argued that death needs life but life does not need death, I hypothesize that wisdom does need experience but experience does not need wisdom. In essence, I have absolutely no proof that I know a damned thing. So what is it exactly that I so desperately need to pass on to my future flakes? What IS life?

Ralph Waldo Emerson said that "Life is a journey and not a destination". This I DO believe.

Apparently, the best thing I can do for my kids before I die is to make sure I leave them the keys to my car.

s

I'm not saying Native Indians are gay.

I try, as a general rule, not to pay attention to the news unless I have particular reason to fear that I'm going to be featured on it as part of a horrible surprise expose. When I have had the misfortune to catch the occasional glimpse into that wildly slanted offering, facetiously called "reporting", I've noticed a recurring theme of heavy debate over the issue of Gay Rights. I find it comical to consider, with all of the issues in the world today, that this one ranks as front page news that needs to be urgently spread to the public and openly debated.

I honestly have no idea what the actual core issues of this debate are because my wife has instructed me to refrain from homosexuality due to whatever drunken commitments we made in our own matrimonial promises. So involving myself in the issue has seemed like a moot point for me. Honestly, even if I weren't married, I've been told that I don't have the fashion sense or tidiness to be gay.

From what I understand, same sex marriage is an important debate for EVERYONE because it establishes a legal precedence of government involvement in private relations between consenting adults. This a debate that could, by similar standards, possibly start with gender and then proceed to dictate acceptable ranges of age, race, religious background, or even end up legislating the sale of peanut butter to lonely people with dogs.

I can see possibly legislating bi-sexuality because that is just plain greedy. It makes for monopolies, like Microsoft had. Clearly the government needs to intervene there. But as for HOMO-sexuality, well, that seems pretty innocuous to me. If the government is continually allowed to screw EVERYBODY, we should be allowed to choose at least ONE person for ourselves to screw. It seems only fair.

On a seemingly unrelated point, I've often wondered how many things did Native Indians smoke before they discovered marijuana? How many Injuns needlessly perished from smoking poison ivy first?

To bring that thought into relative homosexual debate, consider the dandelion. It reproduces through a germination process much akin to the human sneeze. I'm not sure that dandelions have specific genders because I think there would have to be a plant called a dandelioness for that to be the case. But let's assume for a minute, that through the process of elimination, much like Indians smoking poison ivy, that humans once tried reproducing through sneezing instead of through coital contact. Soon humans found, that although sneezing felt GREAT, this "oralgasm" was not a viable method for reproduction.

However some people continued to be born with allergies and prone to involuntary or even voluntary bouts of sneezing. Let's say then that the government makes it illegal to sneeze. I don't suspect that law would affect the needs of the body or the impulses of the mind of the person with allergies. It is what it is. Further, the government decides that the dandelion is not as pretty as other flowers and decided to weed it out of our collective yard. But pulling weeds makes more people sneeze....

And then the Indian is left standing in his garden wondering why the hell the government is screwing up his land while he is just trying to chill out with his doobage.

I think that is what happened here. I'm not saying Indians are gay. Or that they smoke weed. Or that I would have sex with an Navajo man. I'm just saying I heard there was a debate.

Let's talk about your Mother

Whenever I complained about anything as a child, my mother would simply reply "Boy, you'd complain if they hung you with a new rope". I never really understood that, because hanging seemed legitimately bad enough that the type of rope shouldn't really seem to be a primary concern. I'd actually prefer a really old weathered rope with so much fraying that it would just break under the tremendous strain of my fatness, and that I'd just land safely on the ground saying something like "Thank God that wasn't one of them fancy new ropes". But I think the point of that ridiculous saying was SUPPOSED TO BE that some people complain about everything.

Nine of out ten people see something like a cute baby and say: "Awww, how sweet!" and the tenth guy says: "That thing is loud and it's going to poop on my carpet". Some people work multiple minimum wage jobs, win a million dollar lottery, and then complain about taxes. I can't count the number of times that I thought someone was going to pull out a gun and start shooting over something trivial like not getting pickles on their sandwich at McDonald's. When you see a ridiculous behavior like this, you have to think: "This person CAN'T really be this upset over pickles. Maybe they just haven't been able to poop for the last three months. There HAS to be some other source for this rage." My immediate response when I see someone freaking out in public over nothing at all is: "Why is it legal to euthanize my dog for biting the mailman but not legal to lethally inject a human that wants to have a fist fight with a 16 year-old kid over pickles at McDonald's?". Laws are so silly sometimes.

Apparently the right thing to do when you see someone freaking out is to assume that something else legitimate is bothering them and that they are merely venting that frustration here. You should "put yourself in their shoes" for a while. Personally, if I was in their shoes, I would walk myself up the platform, stick my own neck in the noose and then call out to the executioner "Hey fat boy, nice rope! Is this the leash you use to take your mom for walks?" I'm pretty sure that would get me killed, and frankly, I'd think that was the best thing for me. If my life ever devolves into fighting over pickles, I'm going to see if I can slip my local veterinarian a twenty dollar bill to go ahead and put me to sleep.

The truth is that everyone really does have a deeper underlying source of animosity. A lot of psychiatrists say that behavior is related to the relationship you have with your mother. Perhaps that is why I've been trained to believe that insulting an executioner's mother will facilitate a more immediate demise. I don't know if it's a presumed generalization based on genetics or if it's rooted in the fact that she is the person who was supposed to spend 18 years slapping the back of your head when you disrespected others, I just know that a lot of therapy sessions start with the words "Let's talk about your mother...". I find that connection to be very odd because I've tried, very unsuccessfully, to use this same psychology myself when faced with angry strangers in awkward social situations. I started out with simple genetic research questions that might help me understand the root of the person's frustration, like "Excuse me sir, but is your mother socially inept too?". I even tried adding humor to the questions but "Your mama" jokes just seem to make angry people even madder. I'm not sure exactly how that psychology is supposed to work. I have heard the Sigmund Freud did a lot of cocaine so there is the chance that his research was a little rushed. With enough cocaine, a guy could feasibly write an entire thesis in fifteen minutes. I'd guess that leaves some margin for error.

Clearly, I am not an expert on human behavior. Creating dialogue about other people's mothers has proven repeatedly to be an ineffective tool for understanding their behaviors. Still, as an adult male, I have an innate need to answer life's questions and have resolution, at least in my own head. Therefore, the ONLY way I know to handle this situation is to handle it the way I handle other problems with answers that seemingly cannot be revealed. I create additional new conflict that agitates the person until they finally cave inward and can reveal the true source of conflict for themselves. Conflict can be a psychology of its own. By creating bigger problems, you can solve smaller problems. We use this practice at work all the time so I'd guess it MUST be the right thing to do.

If I see a guy screaming in line about pickles, I try to do something subtle while his focus is elsewhere. It may be something small, like stealing his wallet, or slashing his car tires, or it may be something bigger, like suddenly shanking him in the kidney with a plastic spork. Either way, by upping the ante, my actions have frequently been proven to provide the angry person with the true source of his agony. I'd say at least half the time I do this, the angry person ends up on the floor, crying, and curled up in the fetal position whimpering reflectively. "Geez man, all I wanted was to eat lunch and go back to work, but nooooo...instead I get fired, go home to find my wife in bed with the neighbor, and when I do finally get a sandwich, it has no pickles..." And thus, the true problem is revealed. Free therapy.

I could probably employ deeper psychology to explore the issue further and say something like "Yeah, I bet your mom likes pickles.". But I don't. Sometimes a simple shanking is enough. But just to be sure, I always keep a new rope in the trunk of my car.

The beef jerky fairy

I went to Meijer this morning to get food and hair product to sculpt my armpit hair. I was outside waiting for a car to back out and I was going to take their parking spot. An older woman who was making eye contact with me came right in from the other side and took my spot. Not cool.

Once inside the store, I spotted her rounding the first corner so I gave chase. As I headed down the first aisle, I saw a plastic display strip on the wall that had $5.99 bags of peppered beef jerky hanging off of it. I took the whole strip. I passed the woman in the second aisle and slyly deposited two bags of beef jerky into her shopping cart. I passed her again on the next aisle and added two more bags. I couldn't get any more in until we reached the back of the store near the cheese, where I finally had a chance to slip the seven remaining bags of beef jerky into her cart. That's $66 in beef jerky if you are counting.

We reached the checkout lane at the same time and I was one line away from her. She realized that she had a LOT of beef jerky in her cart and went to put it back. I reloaded her unattended cart with Trident "SPLASH" bubble gum and a People magazine with Patrick Swayze on the cover.

I have no idea what the purpose of this whole ordeal was but it brought me a strange joy, like covert government agents must experience on occasion. I'm hoping that whomever was manning the video cameras on the ceiling was at least enjoying my work. I also hope that the lady with the cart lies awake at night wondering if she has some kind of deep seeded subconscious need for beef jerky that she needs to be aware of.

I wish I had time to follow her around the rest of the day and make her think that she is going crazy. Sometimes people need that in their lives so that they can shift their focus off of being mean to strangers in parking lots.

Everybody is gonna die

Every once in a while, I take six or seven seconds to reflect on my own mortality...usually as a result of something terrible I've eaten. It's not uncommon for me to attempt suicide with food, not because I hate life, but because I LOVE food. Besides, when you get right down to it, Life itself, is a terminal illness. Everybody is gonna die. So really, what's the harm in a giant country fried chicken smothered in white gravy sitting beside a loaded baked potato, and washed down with Kahlua spiked milkshake? A heart attack at a table like that still beats the hell out of a fatal six year battle with hiccups or Chlamydia. If I ate salads all the time and ran marathons,

I'd surely get hit by a car. Sometimes you have to throw caution to the wind and just live your life.

However, my carelessness and indifference is frequently betrayed by my whimsical need to die correctly and with as much cool factor as humanly possible. I'm not sure why. I think it started with the fact that I'm a big music fan. I always liked the group INXS and the singer, Micheal Hutchence, had a great charismatic presence. He was the kind of guy that could have slept in a van for a week without showering and still have sex with your mom if he wanted to. He was that cool. Until...he was found dead in a hotel room hanging from his own belt with his pants around his ankles. Death by auto erotic asphyxiation...or simply put...Choked out while choking his own chicken. For a modern day Romeo, that was a really horribly lame way to die. I always figured he'd be ravaged to death and eaten by Amazon women. He deserved better.

So whenever I fly airplanes, or skydive, or mountain bike, or try to beat Kristie Alley in an eating contest, I always do it pretty fearlessly. If I were to die while doing something like that, it's okay. It's like the Fonz getting killed jumping a motorcycle over a swimming pool full of sharks. Beats the hell out of anal cancer right?

But if I'm doing something horrible, like putting clothes pins on my nipples and dancing to Menudo records, I always stop and think...this would be a terrible time to die. There is a shame there. Ask Elvis. The first King of Rock died pooping on the toilet. Granted, they say it was like a 34 pound turd he was trying to pass which is kingly indeed, but still not the way he wanted to go I'm sure.

So yesterday morning my Greyhound had a massive seizure. She just started flipping around the hallway and into the bedroom like a frog on crack. I didn't really know what was happening at first. I figured maybe she ate a live chicken and was trying to poop it out. She does stuff like that sometimes. Then I realized that this was a more serious event. I actually thought she was dying. It was not fun to watch...

However, when the seizure became strong enough, our dog began to fire fully formed balls of poop out of her rectum like a we were taking pitches in a batting cage. Poop was flying everywhere like fireworks at Disney. Crazy stuff. I've witnessed some horrible diarrhea in my time on Earth but I've never seen projectile pooping in solid form before. Pretty impressive actually. I'm not sure that I personally have the ass muscles to pull of something like that.

I tend to remember strange things from my past...like graffiti in a Waffle House men's room when I was a kid that read "Anyone can pee on the floor... but it takes a real hero to poop on the ceiling". Well, by those standards, my dog was being downright heroic. Thankfully it did not kill her.

Just to be near her, I ended up sleeping on the couch that night. I was pretty beat from a night of competitive dodge ball (another very honorable way to die) anyway so I'm not so sure I that I even could have made it bed. I fell asleep watching an infomercial about brownie pans and fondling myself in amazement of the potential for better snacking (a much less honorable way to die). Around 3 AM, I woke up with a gigantic Charlie Horse in my left calf. Ironic that I would have a horse inside a calf huh? That's like stuffing Duck inside chicken (which I totally dig) but I digress. A Charlie Horse is an ungodly muscle spasm that makes your leg feel like it's trying to give birth to a walrus. I woke up as the pain was just reaching the "Sweet Jesus, I've just kicked myself in the back of my own head" level, and was then fully awake as the pain progressed to the "I think I've just tied my own knee in a knot" level.

I leapt from the couch like a drunk man who had just peed in an electric blanket and began to dance around the room on one leg while screaming obscenities like Satan himself, IF he had Turret's Syndrome. Just as I began to cry, I thought to myself..."thankfully this is just my leg". I was actually relieved. I wasn't having a full blown seizure like my dog. Apparently those aren't totally contagious. But I thought to myself, this would be a terrible way to die. Kicking myself in the back of my own head is uncool enough but if I would have had a full on seizure while pleasuring myself to brownie infomercials and then proceeding to projectile poop in my own living room, well....that would be downright embarrassing.

It's 3:30 in the morning and my leg still hurts like hell. I'm going to bed. I'll part with a traditional epileptic farewell....I'll Seizure Later Guys!

The revolving door of torment

My life is a revolving door of torment between my good intentions and my bad deeds. Because I have had nine broken bones in the last four months, I've become increasingly aware of my changing physique due to inability to exercise like I pretended to do before. So instead of my usual breakfast of chocolate chip pancakes and nutty bars, I decided to go to the store today and purchase some oatmeal for breakfast. While, there I even purchased some vegetables and, in an unplanned act of kindness, grabbed some stuff to make a casserole for my lovely bride and our two and a half offspring so that they would not have to fend for themselves while I was at work tonight, surrounding myself with bountiful portions of tasty fresh food.

I came home and went right on the one-hour task of preparing the ideal casserole for the family. I even went so far as to bake some cookies for the girls since I had the oven already hot. Of course, I turned on the television during the whole affair because I have ADD and need at least sixteen different things going on at all times. I became quickly entranced in the show "Masterminds" and absent-mindedly microwaved last night's lasagna, which I ironically didn't finish during last night's similar effort to not continually be a fat ass. I wolfed it down in like two bites and then decided it was best to leave the kitchen and its inherent temptations. I set the timer for the cookies while letting the casserole cool and blocked off the kitchen entrance from the dogs. I adjourned to the office to check my e-mail and surf the web for car porn.

Of course, I began watching silly videos on YouTube because of that whole ADD thing and cranked the sound waaaaaay up to enjoy the spectacles in full audio glory. About eight minutes into one par-ticular video, I heard an inexplicable beeping.

"OH GOD!" I thought to myself, I forgot about the cookies!

I leapt from my chair and raced down the hallway with four, yes four, dogs chasing my feet in obvious anticipation of sharing in what-ever greatness had suddenly inspired me into such fervent action. I hurdled the dog fence in a graceless bound and left the quadrupeds crying at the gate. I swung open the oven door just in time to see my cookies teetering on the brink of becoming just a shade too brown. Realizing there was not a single second to wait, I reached into the three-hundred-seventy-five degree oven with my bare hands and rescued the tray of M&M Peanut Butter cookies in the last possi-ble split second where golden perfection could still be achieved. My hands were burned on the dutifully and well thought out stone bak-ing tray purchase, and I did not so much as utter a single whimper. I knew that any good hospital could fix my hands but there was NO ONE who could resurrect a burned cookie. I had made the right call.

Basking in the newfound goodness of cookie salvation, I instinc-tively reached to reward myself and this dizzying physical effort with a huge piece of the now perfectly cooled casserole that was sitting on the counter, just an ironically placed arms length away. The amazingly golden baked cheese capped casserole was heavy in my wounded hands but I hoisted it like a bejeweled crown and crammed it into my mouth with the joy that a baby cow finds warmth in the shelter of warm barn in the dead of winter. Mmmmmmmm..... sweet baby cow...er...casserole.....SOOOOO TASTY. I couldn't stop at just one piece. I ate what I would estimate to be two pounds of casserole in what couldn't have lasted more than two minutes of pure unadulterated feeding frenzy. I don't know what happened to cause this but I was suddenly shamed.

I frantically searched for a container that was big enough to entomb the remaining casserole and place it into the cryogenic chamber for later revival. To my amazement, I owned not a single piece of Tupperware strong enough or massive enough to contain even the remaining amounts of casserole. What to do??? I briefly pontificated consuming the remaining few pounds of casserole simply because it would be a sin to waste it. But I was already stuffed...REALLY stuffed. Should I? Could I? Would I? NOOOOOOO!!!! Resistance was difficult but I split the remaining portions onto heavy ceramic plates and tucked them into their temporary round beds and covered them gently with massive foil blankets before placing them in the refrigerator and out of harm's way.

Finally, I turned and saw that I had orphaned the freshly baked cookies. I saw them sitting all by themselves on the counter, looking all sad and golden brown and fresh. It would be rude of me not to partake in their beauty. I sampled one...then another, then another....

And now here I sit again, trying to stay out of the kitchen, fattened by my efforts to not eat crap all the time. I went to the store in a quest for cholesterol free oatmeal and ended up eating a huge slab of lasagna, a couple pounds of casserole, and untold amounts of cookies because of it. Good intentions....bad deeds. I am the revolving door of torment.

Monkey business

Very few people in this world have had the good fortune to see a human being get beaten up by a monkey. I have had that particular pleasure, not once, but twice. I don't care who you are, this is funny stuff to watch.

I'm normally not a huge fan of child abuse but on rare occasions, and strictly for educational purposes, I make exceptions. In this case, the victim was a little boy, who looked to be approximately 8 years old. Eight years isn't a particularly long time to live on Earth, but it's plenty of time for your parents to teach you basic manners and some simply rules of nature. This boy's parents had obviously failed him that education.

The boy and his annoying sister were in the same pet store as me. We were all customers in case you were wondering. The boy, his sister, and I, were not for sale.

The pet store, however, did have two monkeys for sale. I don't know what kind of monkeys they were. I asked, but the monkeys apparently did not speak English. They weren't very big monkeys though, as judged by me and my vast expertise on all things Monkey. Still, there were large warning signs on the cages, instructing patrons to NOT interact with the animals and to seek managerial assistance if viewing is desired.

Oblivious to the warning signs, the boy and his sister began circling the cage and taunting the poor primates. This quickly advanced into poking and physically antagonizing the monkeys. The store manager asked the children's parents to please not allow this primate abuse to continue.

The parents were worthless and did nothing to help the plight of the poor monkeys. The boy started impersonating the monkey face by puffing up his cheeks and pulling on his own ears while leaning up to the cage. I stopped what I was doing, and gave my entire focus to the unfolding drama. I thought to warn the children but then wisely chose not to. I knew something wonderful was about to happen and stopping it would only have been cheating myself. Instead I waited for ultimate joy to reveal itself to me.

The little caged monkey ran out of patience. He reached his little monkey hands through the bars of the cage and grabbed the boy by his ears. I was impressed when this little tiny monkey lifted the good sized human child completely off of his feet. The boy was hanging from his ears about six inches off of the ground when the monkey began pushing and pulling with a furious speed, like he was bench pressing a rag doll. The boys face would smash off of the cage bars and then he would be thrown back as the monkey extended his arms again. Then the monkey would quickly retract his arms and smash the boys face against the cage again. The process was repeated about 45 times in about sixty seconds. It was a dizzying pace. The sister was crying, the boy was screaming, I was roaring with laughter, the monkey was howling with delight. The pet store was loud. The parents and manager came running but the monkey tossed the boy back to the floor before anyone could intervene. I would have given that monkey a high five if I wasn't so afraid he'd beat me up too.

The other good monkey fight I saw was actually on television the other night. I wish I'd have been there in person but I consider myself highly blessed for having attended one monkey fight already.

There was a group of people on a safari and one of the members was kind enough to record the adventure. When the group encountered a band of gorillas in the wild, the group leader warned everyone to avoid them. One of the tourists apparently deemed himself an expert on gorillas and decided that he would be safe approaching them. The other tourists were yelling that it was not safe to approach the animals.

"It's okay", the man said, as he continued walking, "they don't eat humans."

As video will testify, the man was right. Gorillas do not eat humans. Gorillas will, however, totally and mercilessly beat your ass until they succeed in rendering you into a whimpering bloody soup-like pulp of broken bones and damaged organs, neatly wrapped inside a humiliated and frightened skin bag that was once your body. It was wonderful to watch. The gorilla tossed the man into the air like he had stepped on a land mine. When the man returned to earth, the gorilla began pummeling him with large furry fists, occasionally even backhanding in classic American pimp style to add further insult. It wasn't a one or two punch fight. The monkey had time to spare and was apparently going to be content to spend the remainder of the day beating any future peaceful dreams out this particular man. It was one of the greatest moments in television history and would make a great 3-D movie. The man survived the gorilla beating with some new knowledge. He'll now be the first to tell you; Gorilla's don't eat people, but technically, neither do ninja's. You still shouldn't taunt them.

I recently thought I might be witnessing a third monkey fight at the Indianapolis Motor Speedway but finally had to chalk it up to freakishly hairy humans. I'm still not totally sure but it seems unlikely that an actual gorilla would be wearing a Dale Earnhardt tank top.

Gluttony

Gluttony is one of the deadly sins, sure, but it's also an art. As artists, there is an unspoken bond between people who over eat. Granted, there is competition but at the end of the meal, we are kindred spirits united by a common pursuit. We are recognizable by our stomachs but there are other clues as well. We've been banned from buffets by large signs on the doors of the establishments, and unlike having a bad check posted over the cash register at a retail store, this can be an honor. Perhaps certain restaurants have excluded us by both name and picture in newspaper issued coupons. Maybe we've donated blood, not for the greater good of society, but just to get the free cookie and juice. It's likely that the local pizza place has rented a box truck to deliver our dinners. We've gotten $80 hotel rooms for one hour, not to hide an office romance, but because we were sure we could eat at least $100 worth of complimentary continental breakfast. Rest assured that if someone belches up a live fish after eating seafood, they are indeed, truly gluttons.

If a person is injured while eating, it doesn't mean they have a problem. It could have been a timing issue. They could have been enjoying a low fat snack at the coffee shop when a city bus crashed through the wall and hit them. That's tragic. However, is someone is injured BECAUSE of eating, it's a different story altogether. I have fork scars. That's right, I have scars on my face and hands from where I have actually drawn blood due to inadvertent forking whilst in the midst of feeding frenzy. Anyone who has ever reached for food off of my plate has fork scars too. I don't mess around.

I've got friends and I have friends I eat with. Many times, these are two different groups of people. Many of my "eating friends" are people I would not bring home or allow near my pets. I've done bad things to my body and even the environment with these people. I'm not ashamed of it. Eating competitively takes practice, desire, dedication, wardrobe, and a little bit of natural talent from either God or Satan.

I've eaten 30 White Castle cheeseburgers with my friend Ramaneek. He ate 30 also. Like drinking, it's not a problem if you do it in a social setting. It's when you do it alone or on the job that you've got issues. We called a truce at 30 because neither of us was sure if spontaneous combustion was real or not. Why risk it? White Castles may be small but they are quite potent. They don't serve any other purpose other than to make your pants smell funny. You are better to cut out the middle man by simply licking them and throwing them in the toilet than to actually eat them.

I split 50 one-day-old doughnuts and a gallon of milk with my friend Frank. No crumbs were left. It wasn't a competition. Frank just bought all the doughnuts that bakery had left. We ate them. I don't know why. I do know that 25 doughnuts and a half-gallon of milk are actually bigger inside your body than they are when they are sitting on a bakery shelf. Again, the reasoning eludes me, but I'm quite sure it's true. I still have enough bread in my body that I dry up my pool when I try to go swimming.

I ate over 20,000 calories in one afternoon with Frank and our friend Joe. This time we had a reason. Our high school health class had asked us to track calories for a week. We thought it was like a test where the most points win. We were wrong. It's not easy eating 20,000 calories in an afternoon. It requires several boxes of snack cakes from the Hostess Bakery thrift shop, bags of potato chips, and sandwiches from every major restaurant on Emerson Avenue on the south side of Indianapolis. I'm pretty sure each of set other records later that day in separate bathrooms, but we didn't talk about it. None of us knew about laxatives back then so we just walked around in shame, wearing maternity clothes.

I ate a one cheeseburger, some French fries, and a few pickles with my friend, Murph, in Chicago. I think he took me to this place on purpose. It was a casual roadhouse and the menu was pretty non-descript with the exception of one item at the bottom of the menu that simply said "Betcha-Burger... $25". I had to know more. He knew I would. The Betcha-Burger is a four pound cheeseburger served with two pounds of French fries, three whole pickles and served on an 18 inch pizza tray. The burger was enveloped a very thick, hard French roll and topped with cheeses, lettuce, tomato, pickles, onions, green peppers, mayonnaise, ketchup, mustard and a few other things I could not identify. The burger was cooked in a mere two minutes at a very high temperature which was just long enough to render it as a blackened rim bowl of blood soup. It was not tasty. I ate the meat, the fries, and the pickles but couldn't finish the bun. It was my first defeat ever. It still hurts. I offered $100 to anyone in the place to try to eat just the bun in the 30 minute time period and there were no takers. I'm not sure it was possible.

I ate 22 tacos, a beef burrito and an order of cinnamon sticks at Taco Bell on a dare. We ran out of money at that point. I'm glad. I don't really want to know how much Taco Bell I can eat. I'm a child of the 1980's. I grew up knowing that Russia and the United States each had a big enough arsenal of nuclear weapons to blow up the entire planet 26 times. It was that principle of mutually assured destruction that prohibited each side from ever actually engaging in war. Taco Bell and I have the same understanding. I can eat whatever they make, but the consequences are too intense for either of us to ever really do it.

I ate five McDonald's Big Mac's in fifteen minutes against a guy named Doug. He had talked trash to me all week about how much he could eat. The guy was huge. He literally ate an entire jar of mayonnaise every week at lunch alone. That's a complete jar of mayo every five meals. That can't be good. When it came time to eat, I crushed him. He was weak. I really thought he'd bring a better effort to the table. I ate a large order of fries and two apple pies in that same 15 minutes just to taunt him while he struggled with a mere three Big Mac's. I think his skirt must have been too tight. I will mention that while this was not necessarily a lot of food to eat, I really did think I was having a heart attack about an hour later. I've honestly never been so scared. I had a knot in my chest like I swallowed a boulder. If I did have a coronary episode, it would have been a forfeit. I'm not 100% sure that I didn't actually have a heart attack that day because I didn't go to the hospital. It felt like my heart might have stopped for a while but it started again on its own so I wasn't about to give Doug the victory.

I nearly choked to death on a deep dish pizza as a kid. It wasn't because I ate so much. I think I just didn't chew it. It was scary to stop breathing for such a long time. No one in the restaurant knew the Heimlich Maneuver so one of the patrons just started punching me in the kidneys until I threw up. That did the trick. I spit the pizza about thirty feet. I thought he was a real hero but I think a few other customers threw up right after I did. My kidneys hurt for a few days but I've never been so grateful to take such a beating. In retrospect, I'd bet that guy really did know the Heimlich maneuver but just didn't like kids. He probably doesn't even know that he saved my life. He probably just tells his buddies that one time back in the 1970's he totally beat the hell out of a little blue kid at a pizza place and never got arrested.

Salute to the human butt

Honestly, I don't remember a lot of things from High School. I do remember this though; Ernie Cunningham farted in my freshman English class. I remember that like it was yesterday. Obviously, I'm a sucker for a good tooting of the butt trumpet and I probably dwell on these things more than necessary. This truly was a classic bomb drop though.

Our English teacher had a great way of keeping us all awake during class. We would read stories out loud. Instead of one person reading the others to sleep, each person would read one paragraph and then the next person would read the next paragraph. You had to be alert so that you didn't look like an idiot when it was your turn. I had the misfortune of being seated behind Ernie that day, but I was lucky enough to be one aisle to his right. I saw him squirming as soon as the reading began. I figured he was just nervous about having to read out loud but it turns out that reading was the last thing he was worried about doing out loud.

It started out with a high pitched squeal like someone slowly letting the air out of a helium balloon. It was enough to turn a few heads but not so much as to stop the reading. Ernie kept his head down and pretended nothing was happening but I'm quite sure it was clear to him that the squealing could not continue. Probably wishing it would provide a timely conclusion to the affair, Ernie leaned back in his seat and relaxed his pucker.

The high pitched squeal immediately deepened into a thunderous blast that silenced the readers. The ordeal far from over, Ernie kept his now purple face pointed down at the book on his desk trying not to look conspicuous. At this point though, Ernie was the only one still pretending to read and his intended cover was actually revealing him to be the culprit. Meanwhile, the fart raged on.

In hopes of silencing the thunder, Ernie resorted back to the pucker. The pucker brought back the high pitched squeal. It was very musical, quite like a flute solo, with a sudden burst of accompaniment from a trombone, and then concluding with the flute alone. It was like a Disney soundtrack and seemed to last as long as some of the movies do. I can only imagine the agony for poor Ernie. That fart seemingly had no end. When it did mercifully stop, the conclusion was acknowledged by a rousing ovation of applause from his classmates. Decades later, I'm still impressed. I hold this to be the single fart by which I judge all others.

Farts are a lot like real estate. There are three ways to increase their value: Location, location, and location. Farting at school is funny, but almost expected. Farting at church takes real courage.

Admittedly, I've passed a little gas along with the collection plate in church. I just don't think anyone has ever heard me. I know when the high notes are coming while I'm mouthing the words to the Hymns. I let it go when the choir is the loudest. Even if someone did hear it, I could blame it on old people. There are lots of old people in church trying to make last minute reparations before the dirt nap. It's okay if they fart. They're old. Old people do that.

My friend Jim is a different story. He blatantly cut the cheese at a church breakfast. It was one of the loudest things I've ever heard in my life. Imagine someone trying to sneak a freight train into a library. The table shook beneath my plate. I was in complete disbelief. There was no denying what the sound was. The only question in anyone's mind was whether or not he had used a microphone.

I was sitting next to him at the time. It was the single most shameless fart I've ever heard. It was loud, it was long, it was deep, and it was oblivious to the presence of women and children. It wasn't just a fart. It was an exorcism. It was the devil himself being kicked out of Jim's anus, kicking and screaming all the way. A fart ordinarily doesn't change the temperature in the room. This one did.

I half expected Jim to rise out of his seat and fly around the room like a full balloon that slipped out of someone's hand. Jim's a big guy though, and he remained perfectly seated. He wasn't just seated like a regular person. Jim had actually gone so far as to lift his legs and spread them apart leaving his heels resting on two separate tables before releasing his demon. It was a premeditated church fart. The likes of which had never been seen. It created an eerie silence in the room. It was far beyond audacious. It was the kind of uncomfortable silence that I've come to love.

The next few moments of a silence like that seem to last an eternity. You can literally see the wheels turning inside the minds of the people in the room as they plot the next move to bring appropriateness back to the situation. The next sound uttered or emitted by anyone, through any orifice, is critical. The fate of the future rests upon it. Another fart from anyone else would turn the room into a contest no one wanted to be a part of. An angry word would start a conflict no one wanted at church. Applause would send the wrong message. Collective gasping would require breathing in the polluted air. There was simply no good answer. It was perfect uncomfortable silence that could only be broken by the offender himself.

Jim waited and said nothing.

With both feet still on the breakfast tables and smoke still coming from his pants, Jim looked out at the horrified crowd and pointed to me. "He did it", said Jim.

To me, that was funny. Jim was a study in the art of the perfect delivery. Timing is a critical skill in joke telling and an essential skill in knowing when to stop before you poop yourself when farting. It's all about delivery. The fart was perfect only because of the stunning magnitude and its unparalleled offensiveness. Blaming me afterwards was funny because of how obvious it was that he was the guilty party. Farts like that don't come out of people under 300 pounds. I don't care what you eat. It just doesn't happen. If I had tried to uncork such a monster, I would have literally been blown into little pieces. By the laws of physics, I just couldn't do it. A fart like that would have had to be taken from me in a cesarean fashion. Blaming me was genius. Sadly, no one else appreciated it.

That's the problem with genius. Few people recognize it until after you're dead. That's okay though, as I expect that God will kill Jim just as soon as he figures out where to put him in the afterlife. You can't put anyone that gassy too close to fire. Hell is just not an option.

Dropping bombs

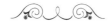

I think that mankind's fascination with bombs is because they are one of the few things on this earth that don't have an exact opposite. You really can't explode anything that will create something besides massive destruction. This makes the phrase "dropping a bomb" a suitable analogy for any serious and sudden event with repercussions that can't be immediately righted. For example, an unexpected and humongous group of extraordinarily obese people descending upon a restaurant without reservations would be the equivalent of "dropping a bomb" on the staff.

Tonight's event began with the bomb drop in the form of this unexpectedly large group of gratuitously plus sized patrons. They were a legitimate challenge to our available resources and it would suffice to say that we were not truly prepared for them.

It was the birthday of the largest man, who is a regular customer of our restaurant. However, claiming exclusivity of this man as a customer would be stretching it, much like calling a prostitute your girlfriend. Sure, he's a regular at our restaurant but I suspect he's also a regular at nearly every other restaurant in the tri-state area. He brought twenty-seven of his friends and family in to the restaurant tonight to celebrate his birthday, which surely is a noteworthy occasion as, medically speaking, he should already be dead. He is not less than 700 pounds and is only in his late twenties.

When I was thirty, I used to joke that I weighed eight pounds when I was born and had gained eight pounds for every year that I had been alive. It would not be quite so funny if I could still say that when I'm sixty. This is not a road map to longevity in life. Even then, I would have to live to be 87.5 years old at that pace to equal the weight this man accomplished in his mere twenties. He seemed to be experiencing an average gain of 40 pounds per year. He was on pace to become his own continent if he reached his eighties. At this rate, he would weigh 3,500 pounds by the time he was 87.5 years old. That's more than my Ford Taurus that I drive on vacation with my entire family and our luggage inside.

Guessing that he is about twenty-eight years old right now at 700 pounds is an interesting comparison to me in another way. I'm fat at 240 pounds according to my doctor and that means that at six foot one, each inch of my height weighs about three pounds. Each inch of this man's height, assuming he is also six feet tall, would weight about ten pounds. That doesn't seem so excessive unless you consider that if wanted look exactly as overweight as I appear, he would need to be nineteen feet tall to still weigh seven hundred pounds. The only real physical difference between us then would be that he was thirteen feet taller and I still wouldn't have dreadlocks or be black. Otherwise, he could be my stunt double.

The man's giant birthday party lasted nearly four hours at seven tables which meant that, unless this party tipped about $400, none of the staff was going to make any money since nearly one-third of the restaurant was devoted to this group for that period of time on a Saturday night. Still, we provided the group with great service and they kept us running for the whole night with their endless consumption of free bread and free drink refills. To make matters worse, I had an upset stomach the whole time and there was never a chance to take a break and use the restroom.

Mercifully, towards the end of the night, the group began to leave and the largest man decided to use our restroom to emancipate many of the food and drink items he had consumed over the last four hours. Our bathroom is very small and has only one standing urinal and one sit down toilet in a separate stall. The large man occupied the stall for a very long period of time as he "gave a little something back to the people who had served him so graciously". I'm sure it was quite an event of its own: A real festival of sights, sounds, and smells. Again, it would be appropriate to describe this as "the dropping of a bomb". There was no offsetting explosion that would undo the carnage that he was creating. Sadly, this did not change the fact that I still desperately needed to use this same bathroom whenever he was finished.

When my turn finally arrived, I had to do some fairly repulsive cleaning before I could do what really needed to be done. The only compensation I would receive for this inhumane cleaning job was that I was finally able to sit down for some much needed and long overdue personal relief, although by this point, I wasn't exactly sure which end of me needed access to the toilet the most. The combination of being physically sick and mentally disgusted left me with the urge to use all available orifices to purge. This was not a good night.

I decided to sit first. I wasn't far into my reward before someone began trying to open the door to my stall. As is customary, I shouted out that the stall was occupied, and followed that statement with the very loud and over acted clearing of my throat that is customary in nonverbally warning others away from your bathroom stall. Still, the door rattled again with the impatient attempt of another to claim my highly coveted real estate. I shouted again that the stall was in use.

I heard a voice reply from the other side of the stall wall.

"I need to go Poo-poo!"

It was a man's voice but clearly not using common vernacular that most adult men use to describe their need to access the bathroom. I was a bit puzzled but I had issues of my own to tend to and further investigation was not really on my mind at the time. My level of curiosity was immediately elevated when I saw the man's fingers grip the top of the stall wall: first one hand, then another. Then I saw the man's head appear like a floating balloon over the top of the wall as he gazed down on me. I could tell by looking that the man was mentally disabled. He had the standard issue mentally challenged eye-glasses and a readily identifiable face that I associate with certain handicaps. That may be wrong to say, but it is accurate. Certain types of mental handicaps leave some adults with an obvious child-like and innocent inherent cuteness that other adults simply don't have.

It occurred to me that the man was either pulling himself up over the wall or he was standing on top of the urinal on his side of the wall. Either proposition was moderately alarming to me but I was so caught off guard with being the focus of his surveillance that I really didn't know how to react.

Then the man swung a leg over the top of the six foot tall stall wall. Just as suddenly, the other leg appeared. Before I could even digest the happenings, the handicapped man was rolling himself over the top of the stall wall and dropping into the very small stall where I was relieving myself. It was not the smooth performance one might expect from an Olympic gymnast but more like...well...a huge handicapped kid falling over a six foot wall onto the lap of an unsuspecting fat guy who had his pants around his ankles and was ill equipped to respond.

The giant man-child rose to his feet and stood before me, smiling. "I'm fourteen", he said.

This was a strange choice of greetings to be sure, but I'm not sure what the normal greeting is after launching yourself into someone else's private toilet area. The next words he spoke seemed to be more of what I was expecting out of his initial remark.

"I need to go Poo-poo", he said.

By this time, I had figured out that fact by myself but it still somehow seemed refreshing to hear exactly what his motives where and to have it come from his own mouth. I was also glad that he was sharing this information with me as a warning rather than just climbing on to my lap and pooping on me. I was in uncharted territory and I don't think that anything I had ever learned in any school prepared me for handling such an occasion.

I would normally think that killing a man is an appropriate response for an intrusion such as this one. At the very least, a savage beating should be issued. That's not really the case when dealing with a severely handicapped person. They tend to earn some privileges that other people don't enjoy. I'm not implying that seeing me on the toilet should be called a privilege but having me accept that observation from a complete stranger certainly qualifies as an indulgence that non-handicapped men would not be allowed.

I did what I thought was best and abbreviated my use of the prized toilet and left the stall in a hurry. I swung the stall door open hurriedly, and was immediately greeted by the exact same face that just staged the hostile takeover of my toilet. An identical twin brother was standing before me, looking equally excited to enter the stall. I immediately wondered how many of these boys there could be. Two? Three? Ten? Was this an invasion of some sort or was I being taped for some part of crazy new reality show?

"Is Carl in there?" asked the second boy.

"Indeed", I replied, "Carl is everywhere."

Once I returned to the restaurant I sat down at a table and began to internalize my feelings. Clearly, I needed some kind of counseling but I was reluctant to share the story with others. I was pretty sure there were laws against my sharing a bathroom stall with an unrelated handicapped minor of the same sex, even if I was not expecting it. It would be kind of like convincing a traffic cop that an unknown naked hooker had skydived into your convertible only moments before you were pulled over for speeding. These things don't happen to normal people.

Still, I was glad that the kid decided to jump into my stall because I've had just enough encounters with insanity to be able to handle the ordeal in a relatively rational and uneventful manner. I can't imagine what would have happened if the wall climbing defecator had hurtled the stall wall just fifteen minutes sooner. He would have been greeted by the site of a 700 pound man perched upon the toilet. The toilet would not have even been visible beneath him and it would have created a monumentally awkward moment of two very large people gathered face to face in a very small room staring at each other with uncertainty and general confusion, like two quadriplegic men at a ping pong table. I also think that given the large size of both people and the fact that door swings into the stall, neither man would have been able to leave. This brings me to my third observation. Firemen and rescue workers don't make nearly enough money.

Speaking of being short-changed, the giant man and his even larger party that occupied our restaurant for nearly fours and single-handedly forever changed the landscape of our bathroom, left us a paltry twelve dollar collective tip for the entire staff to split. We're going to need to spend more than that on bleach for the bathroom.

I'm definitely not paid enough to deal with this type of behavior. I need to find a better second job, and soon. I wonder how much money you make as a private instructor who gives climbing lessons to handicapped people. Obviously there's a market for that.

The worst advice I ever got

I should be dead. My doctor said so. He was talking about my cholesterol but I think if he knew about my jumping construction sites, out drinking famous dead rock stars, eating more than my birth weight in contests, jumping out of airplanes, flying airplanes, crashing mountain bikes, drinking with clowns, fighting homeless people, nearly drowning in elephant snot, bungee jumping, setting houses on fire, setting vans on fire, being in bad car accidents, getting knocked unconscious in a swimming pool, in a parking lot, and on a bicycle, falling from high rooftops, witnessing gang murders, being hit by cars, attacked by dogs, fighting in jail, breaking my head open twice, running from police, falling down large staircases, falling out of trees, falling out of moving cars, or falling off of moving motorcycles, I think my doctor would realize that I'm not going to die of anything normal. I'd be willing to wager that when I die, it will be from either hiccups or an ingrown toenail. I've already had measles.

I think there is a real reason that I am still alive. God has left me here to either learn something really important or to do something really important. The way I see it, if I can continue to avoid those two things, I should live forever.

I have an uncanny ability to extract the hidden messages of life like that.

Despite my temporary immortality, I do remain painfully aware of the subject of death. I lost my mother nine-years ago to cancer and the loss does not subside with time. All of my friends who have passed are still as fresh in my mind as the days we played together. With this in mind, I sometimes feel like I am being watched, not in a guardian Angel kind of way, but more in a disappointed view from the sky kind of way. It's pretty hard to masturbate when you think your mother, all of your dead friends, and the good Lord himself are watching. I'm kidding of course, but those kinds of thoughts do enter my mind whenever I hit someone over the head with a shovel, wrap them in duct tape, stuff them in the trunk of my car, and drive them to a remote forest where I've dug the hole. I'm a little conflicted I guess. I think that's why I'm such a big fan of the medications.

Speaking of remote forests, my dad took me to Eagle Creek Park when I was a kid. We went hiking on the nature trail. When we got far enough away from civilization, my colon conjured up a poop that just wouldn't wait for the trip back to the shelter. I didn't know what to do.

My father informed me that, in nature, it was okay to go to the bathroom anywhere. Ashes to ashes, dust to dust, poop to mushrooms. It's how nature works. I ran behind a tree and made a stinky little place for future mushrooms to grow in. When I finished, I realized that there weren't any toilet paper trees growing in the area. Again, I yelled for my father. Once again, he had an answer.

"Use a leaf", he said.

I did use a leaf. It actually took several leaves to accomplish the task at hand. There are many different types of leaves in the forest but only someone with my luck could unknowingly choose the poison ivy to wipe my butt. I don't just mean dabbing the cheeks either. I sent it deep into the cave.

I didn't figure it out until later that night. I was back at home and watching television when I got an itch in a place I didn't want to send a finger. I tried to ignore it but the itch was just getting started. I started to squirm like asthmatic in a furnace. No amount of squirming would help though. About ten minutes after the itching started, I was flailing about on the floor with both hands down the back of my pants, scratching my ass like it was a lottery ticket.

I didn't care who was watching. There was simply no relief from the relentless itching of my inner cavern. If I had been flexible enough to get my feet back there, I would have been scratching with all fours. My parents were extremely sympathetic and spent crucial minutes laughing hysterically at my sudden agony before finally consenting to help. Help is a relative term since neither of them were willing to scratch the innermost depths of my butt. They offered me a pink bottle of Calamine lotion instead.

They suggested that I pour some of the lotion onto cotton balls and delicately apply it to the affected areas. I didn't have time for that. I popped the top on that bottle and injected the whole thing into the crack of my ass like we were lovers. I sighed, gurgled, bubbled, and gasped for a few minutes before the sweet relief of the pink enema set in. I didn't sleep well that night and my hand didn't smell good in the morning.

The sad thing about having poison ivy in your butt is that the poison ivy doesn't limit itself to just your butt. Mine spread to the next most likely place. It went right on down the hill and up the other side. I had my hands down both sides of my shorts for the next few days. I was running one hand out back through my crack like I was swiping a credit card while the other hand was scratching the front with a vigor that temporarily started a brush fire in my pubic hair. Neither side was appropriate to scratch in public so I just tried not to go in public at all because not scratching was not an option.

I did have to go to school though. Gym class was the worst part. I was keeping a pretty generous protective coating of pink Calamine lotion on my butt and on my genitals and it didn't take long for that pink lotion to turn my pretty white underwear a very unmanly shade of pink.

Pink underwear is a pretty big deal on a guy in middle school. It didn't take long for the other kids to notice it. I'm pretty sure they all thought I was gay. Pleading with them to help me scratch my testicles probably didn't help the matter any. I'm not sure how long I had the poison ivy but I know it went away before I learned about suicide or I wouldn't be here today. I'm still pretty careful about what plants I put in my butt.

A little secret

I'm sometimes amazed at the secrets people keep from even their very best friends. There are some secrets that people should definitely take to the grave with them, and I recognize that. There are also some secrets that should have been shared long ago.

My roommate in college used to say that he was going to take tap dancing lessons for about five years and not tell anyone. Then one night at a bar, he was going to get up on the bar and, I quote, "tap his little heart out". He then planned to spend the rest of his life denying that it ever happened and that everyone was just drunk and imagining things. I thought that seemed like an awful lot of work for a one time joke. There is an easier way to shock your friends. I know because I've seen it done.

I was at a concert with a good friend of mine. I've known him since birth and our parents were friends even before us. I really thought I knew everything about this guy. The concert was a Heavy Metal Reunion of the big haired 1980's bands. It was great. There were tons of people in the crowd who literally had not changed since the 1980's. When I say they hadn't changed, I mean they hadn't even changed clothes. The outdoor concert was like walking into a time warp back to 1984, and we had a lawn seat view of the whole affair.

There was one particular person who had my attention in the crowd. He had the same mullet haircut that he'd had in the 1980's; business in the front, party in the back. He had a 1984 Ratt concert T-shirt on with the sleeves ripped off, tight blue jeans, unlaced high top basketball shoes, and bandanas tied around his ankles. He had both hands raised up over his head giving the devil horns with his fingers and he was banging his head to the music for a solid hour. He was also a midget.

The fact that he was a midget shouldn't have been an issue. I'm sure it wasn't by choice and it certainly wasn't reason to ridicule the man. I did though. I'm not a very good person, especially when I'm drinking. I leaned over to my buddy and mentioned he should have a look at the little head-banger. My buddy was a better person than I and he failed to see the humor in it. I spent the next several minutes quietly contemplating if I was indeed being juvenile by finding this scenario to be amusing. I decided that I was being immature, and that he should have been more immature too. I pointed the man out again and this time I made sure to specifically address the diminutive stature of the man by saying "Did you, or did you not, see the midget?" I was rightfully ignored by my friend.

Several minutes passed before my buddy leaned back over to me and said the four words I will never forget.

"I had a midget."

It took a minute for the words to sink in, and when they did, I was even more confused. What exactly does "I HAD a midget" mean? "Uh, pardon me?" I asked.

The answer was the same.

"I had a midget", he said, quite casually while still looking at the band and listening to the music.

"Had, as in...... sexually?" was my next inquiry.

Still quite casually, he responded, "Well, dwarves actually. If that counts.".

My mind was racing now. Dwarves? Plural? A guy I have known all of my life has had sex with multiple dwarves and failed to mention it until just now? How can this happen? Honestly, this should have come up in conversation at some point. It was obvious that my friend did not think that midgets or dwarves were funny or unusual, and apparently seemed to think that everyone had experienced multiple sexual encounters with them. I'm not knocking dwarves here, because apparently that is his job, but I felt more than a little slighted at that point. Not only had my friend been having sex with dwarves, but apparently everyone else had too? Prior to this conversation, I thought this was an event reserved for people who lived in hollow trees and made cookies. Where had I been? Are dwarves not attracted to me? Had I ever actually even seen a dwarf? Is this what people mean when they say they hope to "get a little"? So many questions....

It turns out that the dwarves were twin sisters and the sex was all in one crazy night of short, hot passion. Later, he tried to sleep with the girls' mother. It didn't work out. Our lifelong friendship began to decay that day and isn't anything close to what it used to be. I blame the secret for that. When I see a friend once a week for my entire life, it should not take years to mention that he tried to, and had halfway succeeded, bed multiple generations of the same family and that all of them were dwarves? I'm sure he told me something trivial like what movie he had seen that weekend. How did this small detail of the weekend events slip through the cracks only to surface years later in a casual conversation at a rock concert? Again, I guess he just didn't think it was a big deal. It wasn't. It was two small deals. Besides, dwarves look just like any other girls. They just appear to be a little farther away. I'll get over it.

Fairly pedestrian

Now that I have beseeched you to be good and holy, the time just feels right to tell you about some of the people I have hit with my car. To date, I've hit three pedestrians. I'm sure that's an accurate number because you tend to not forget these things. I think the first one is always the most special. Mine was no exception. I remember that she had a cane.

I was minding my own business while drag racing my friend Greg down a major street here in town. We had both gotten off of work at the local mall, and his Chevy Camaro and my Monte Carlo were pretty evenly matched. We raced from stoplight to stoplight for about a mile and we were just waiting for this light to turn green so that we could race to the next light. The light turned green and we both stomped on the go pedals in our respective cars. As usual, it was a close race as we approached the next stoplight but the light turned yellow and I wasn't sure that either of us would get stopped before it turned red. We both skidded to a stop just slightly into the intersection. Both cars over ran the painted pedestrian crossing line in the street by several feet. This was a crime that did not go unnoticed.

There was a lady getting ready to cross the street when we stopped. As mentioned, the lady had a cane to help her walk. Right now you probably have some horrible idea that I was about to run down an old lady with a walker. You would be wrong....sort of. Yes, I did run her down, BUT I don't think she was really that old. In fact, she was probably only in her mid-fifties and I'll be the only reason that she even had that walker was because she'd been in some kind of debilitating accident...like say, maybe, being hit by a car.

Anyway, she began to cross the street in front of us, but not without screaming and pointing to the pedestrian line that we had crossed. She passed in front of Greg's car first and gave him an earful to match the dirty, evil eye that she was giving him. Then she hoisted her cane up into the air and slammed it down onto the hood of Greg's car.

WHAT?!?! I would have no part of this Tom Foolery!

So as this little lady approached my car and began reading me the riot act too, I gave her a warning. I lifted one finger, and no, it wasn't that finger. It was my index finger. I shook it from side to side to tell her no. Then I put one foot on the brake and the other on the gas. The car lifted slightly in the rear and the rear tires began to spin but because I had the brake depressed the car was not moving. This should send the message, I thought.

The evil little lady pressed on, undeterred by the raw power of my manly Monte Carlo. Her cane rose into the air, casting a shadow of doom onto the hood of my prized chariot. It was precisely at this moment, that my left foot slipped, and I swear...it slipped, off of the brake pedal. My right foot, however, had no problem maintaining its original task of mashing the gas pedal to the floor. This created a fairly immediate problem as the car launched with the woman standing directly in front of it. It's not really fair to say that hit her. We were already touching when I moved. It's a matter of semantics really. She wasn't so much hit by a car as she was just...say...maybe suddenly ushered into a more horizontal position ....courtesy of a 3800 pound vehicle.

I knew she was okay because she got right up and started screaming and shaking her cane again. I could see it all very clearly in my rear view mirror as I raced to the next light. Neither I, nor the evil little hag, had learned a thing. I'm not sure who won the races between Greg and I but I'm pretty sure that I know who won between the cane and the Monte Carlo bumper.

The second person I hit remains my favorite strike to date. I never liked this guy. Not many people did. I had the chance to hit him and I took it. No regrets. I will say that I learned the most from this incident. I was still in high school and I had a bad habit of sleeping through my physics classes. If I'd have stayed awake for those classes, I probably would have learned how little force it takes an automobile to really move an object of much lighter mass. Knowing what I know now, I probably wouldn't have hit this particular pedestrian nearly as hard as I did. Alas, I was not as knowledgeable then, so I plowed this kid pretty good.

I saw him standing in the street in front of my girlfriend's house and we made eye contact while I was nearly a block away. He knew where I was going to park in front of her house so he went and stood in the street to block me. What a silly boy. I was only going about three or four miles per hour when I approached him. When I made the decision to hit him, I realized I would need much more speed to knock down such a big kid. I floored it at the last minute. I'd guess that I was still going maybe 5 MPH when I first hit him. I'd guess I was going about 7MPH when he went across the hood. I think my speed had improved to about 10MPH when his face hit the windshield and I feel comfortable estimating a solid 15MPH when he went over the roof and off the trunk back into the street. It was pure poetry as far as hitting pedestrians goes.

This was my first intentional strike and it was pretty stupid. I could have easily killed this kid. But I didn't. And as we've learned, NEAR death experiences are hilarious. I've heard this kid is still every bit as annoying as he was when I struck him down so I feel no remorse whatsoever. The bonus here is that, while I can't even remember what this guy really looked like, I can remember the funny expression on his face when it hit my windshield. It would have made a dandy yearbook picture.

My third strike was another elderly person. This time he was legitimately old and not some poser who was merely crippled and trying to look old like the first lady I hit. This incident still warms my heart because it was part of such a wonderful human interest story. Frankly, I was glad to be a part of it.

The story began after college when I took a job with a law firm in downtown Indianapolis. I spent a lot of time walking the street from courthouse to courthouse and law firm to law firm. I quickly got to recognize and even know many of the zany characters on the streets of downtown Indy. One man was a belligerent drunk that everyone seemed to like pretty well. He asked me one day if he could "borrow" ten dollars and I, for whatever reason, gave it to him. Obviously, I knew that I wouldn't be getting that money back and that I was probably just helping to keep him drunk for another day. Here's where the story takes an interesting turn.

Months later I saw this same man again on the street. This time he was all cleaned up and appeared to be sober. He remembered me, and thanked me for the ten dollars I had given him months before. Then the man reached into his pocket, pulled out a ten dollar bill, and gave it back to me. It seems that after I gave him the money the first time, some guys mugged him and beat him nearly to death. This should have been hilarious, because he didn't actually die. We've talked about this before. It's funny if no one gets killed. That's what makes it a NEAR death experience. But I liked this guy and he was already at the end of his rope so it wasn't very funny.

The upside is that he quit drinking because he didn't have any money after the robbery and eventually got a job as a courier for a law firm. I'm happy to say that he was still doing well the last time I saw him years later. This story gave me a renewed hope and interest in street people, beggars, and those who are publicly intoxicated and wandering the streets during regular business hours.

Unfortunately, my next experience didn't have such a happy ending. I was walking down the street to the courthouse when an old man approached me. He said something to me in a voice so soft that I couldn't even hear him. I asked him to repeat himself and he very clearly restated that he would give me $100 to perform sex acts upon him. This was not the comment I was expecting from a man who probably went to high school with Jesus. He was old...really old...like Yoda. Honestly though, I couldn't blame him for wanting sex acts from me. I was hot. So I politely declined his offer and turned to walk away. That's the moment where the old man grabbed my butt.

I was actually stunned at this point. While it was definitely the most action I'd seen in a while, I felt like the prehistoric man had crossed the line. I also felt that if sex was worth a hundred bucks, he should already be forking over at least ten bucks for this.

Punching a man who was more than 650 years my senior, while standing in front of a Federal Courthouse, seemed like a sure way to get arrested. I truly had no response for this. I felt like a bit of my manhood had been taken away that day.

About a week later I was driving in to work on the very same street where I had once hit a lady with a cane. This street was simply a very suitable place for striking pedestrians with automobiles so you shouldn't be surprised at what happened next. It's a one way street that is six lanes wide heading into downtown at this particular location. I saw that dirty old man walking down the sidewalk on my side of the street. If I'd have been in any of the five other lanes, I couldn't have gotten to this man. It was as if I was supposed to hit him. The planets were aligned and the message was clear.

The goal wasn't to actually hit him. That would be both illegal and unwise given the vast number of witnesses in that morning's commute. I didn't feel like there was anything wrong or illegal about giving him a good scare though. The light changed and I gave my little economy car all the gas it had. As I approached him, I gave a well timed swerve to the sidewalk. Again, the goal here wasn't to make contact. Obviously I did though or I wouldn't be telling you this story right now.

I believe hunters call what I did "winging their prey". It was not a direct or fatal hit, but rather a glancing blow that spun the man around like a ballet dancer before dropping him on his ass. I had hit him only with the mirror on the passenger side of my car but apparently I got him right in the hand. It was the butt-grabbing hand too, which made the victory twice as sweet. I couldn't have done that if I tried.

Illegal?

You betcha.

Witnesses?

Plenty.

Did I stop?

Not on your life.

I spent the rest of the day and most of the week in fear. I was simply waiting for someone to call the police and for the police to come to the law firm and escort me out in handcuffs. They never did. One thing did come after me though. That thing is called Karma.

Greatest hits

I believe that we were just discussing karma. Since I just devoted a whole chapter to people I've hit with my cars, now would be a good time to discuss the people who have hit me with their cars. This is how karma works. It's no mystery. I had a few coming.

The first person to ever hit me with a car was my own father. It wasn't any form of punishment or anything like that. It was simply a case of him leaving without me and me running out to catch him while he was backing down the driveway. Apparently I thought my leg could stop a moving car. I learned that it can't. Cars can roll right over people. I advise everyone to make a note of that.

The second time I got hit, it was much more exciting. It was part of a police chase downtown and it occurred only weeks after I struck the old man. Karma was getting faster.

I was walking to the courthouse again on a Friday afternoon. I was reading a document because I was interested in other people's private business and because it was a great way to avoid conversation from people that I was pretending not to see. I looked up to make sure that I had the light for pedestrian right of way before I crossed the busy street. The light ensured me that it was safe to go. The light was wrong. I was about half of the way across the street when I heard squealing tires. I looked up just in time to see that I was about to get hit by a car. There was no question about it.

The car was turning the corner and the driver was looking back over his shoulder. This was a good sign to me that he would not be swerving or stopping. I tried to run but only got about one step into it before getting hit. The bumper clipped my knee but the front tire hit my leg and threw me to the street with a real sense of purpose. I hit the street hard. I knew it was hard because I could hear the collective "OOOOOOOOOH!!!!!" from the crowd of about 90 people at the bus stop on the corner as I went down. It wasn't pretty. I had a few broken bones and literally had tire tracks on a nice new pair of pants. The man didn't stop to see if I was okay but I didn't blame him. I never stop either. It would be hypocritical to blame him for that.

One of the many reasons this man didn't stop is because he was driving a stolen car. The reason that he was looking back over his shoulder while turning was because he was watching the police car that was chasing him around the corner.

The police car stopped to help me when I got hit, and the man in the stolen car got away. Supposedly, the car had been stolen from a nun that was visiting a prisoner at the jail down the street. If that is true, it explains a lot. If you are going to steal, you might as well steal from a nun. If you are going to run from police, you might as well hit a pedestrian on your journey. When you are on a roll like this guy, you probably shouldn't stop for anything.

The funny thing is that the officer didn't actually see me get hit. So when he asked the 90 or so people at the bus stop who would be willing to be a witness, not one of them admitted that they saw what happened. These are probably the same tight-lipped people who saw me strike the old man weeks before. At least they weren't playing favorites. This goes back to my theory that other people's interest in you extends only as far its affect on them.

The real tragedy to this story is that it was 4:30 on a Friday afternoon when I got hit. Sure it was Workman's Comp Claim since it happened on the clock but I was out of the hospital the same night and back at work on Monday morning. I just wish the guy would have had the common decency to hit me around 8:30 on a Monday morning. Really, some people just have no manners at all.

If you are keeping score, I'm up 3 to 2 in the pedestrian strikes. I've still got one coming.

Three dogs

I have three dogs. They cost me a lot of money each year and I sometimes ask myself, why do I have pets? It's a common practice in America but a mystery in other parts of the world where pets would be meals. For me, the reason is simple. I'm a loser and I need to be the boss of someone. I've tried simply keeping hostages at the house but apparently there are laws about that stuff. Pets are different. You can confine them indefinitely and no one says a thing. Another advantage over hostages is that you can drag your pets down the street on a chain that's wrapped around their neck. Try that with a person and see what happens.

On the other hand, people don't generally poop in your living room. So it's a give and take situation really.

When I was single I got my first dog, Chili. Everyone needs a Chili dog. It's gone downhill from there. When I was a single man, I ruled the house. Chili is a girl. As everyone knows, once you have one woman in your life you are outnumbered.

It happened quickly from there. Within five years, I was married to one woman, had two daughters, two female dogs, eleven fish, and not a penis to be found other than my own penis, which is the one that caused the whole mess. Finally we got a male Rottweiler and my wife promptly had his balls removed. This procedure is called neutering. Again, this is something you do to animals because the law wouldn't let her do it to me.

The worst thing about the neutering is that my wife made me take our Rottweiler in for the deed to be done. The dog's name is Big Boy but his Mafia name is Larry the Eyebrow. We're close so I just call him Larry. I've been close to a few guys in the past and that isn't nearly as gay as it sounds. What I'm saying is that I have what I'd call good male friends that I've been through some tough times with. But I've never, and I mean never, had to take any of those guys in to get their balls cut off. So I was more than a bit reluctant to do this with Larry. I only did it because my wife uses mind control on me like all wives tend to do when they need something or want to send a message.

The fateful day came, when Larry and his balls were separated. As men, both of us were sad. I'm not sure where his balls ended up but I tell Larry that they are in a traveling display sponsored by the Guinness Book of World Records and that seems to make him feel better. It could be true. I don't know. But I do know that I'd want to be told that if I woke up and my balls were missing. It would help keep the machismo intact I think.

Anyway, in the months following the neutering, Larry plumped up from about 90 pounds to about 120 pounds. I was worried and I called the vet. The vet didn't really offer any explanation but said it was to be expected. I have my own theories. Larry really liked to lick those things and spent a lot of time and energy vigorously running around in circles to have a go at them. Those days are gone now.

These days he just lies down and licks his own paws. There is simply no cardio benefit in the new program.

My third dog, Bella, is a Greyhound. She is simply the most neurotic creature on the planet. She serves no purpose at all except to run through the house at supersonic speeds and to stop occasionally to eat various non-food items like our carpet and our curtains. She once ate an entire table cloth. The table cloth was red. I know this for a reason. There was not a shred of table cloth left as evidence and I would have probably never known that she was the reason it was missing...except that I was in the backyard a day later when her body figured out it wasn't food. The table cloth had made its way through the usual bodily channels and was being served its eviction notice when she began to cry. I didn't know what was happening but she was yelping and scooting around the back yard at a high speed with her front two legs peddling hard and her rear legs and butt were just dragging on the grass. I wasn't sure what to make of it. Then I saw something red. Whatever it was, it was hanging about ten inches out the back door of this dog. I needed a closer look. The dog was not eager to show it off and clearly, the process was not going well for her. She was in a lot of pain.

Once I figured out that it wasn't her lower intestines or any other required organ, I slipped the gloves on and the rodeo began. I finally got a hand on the mystery tail and the dog ran one way and I ran the other. My hand slipped off of the prize though and I saw Bella running with what was now about 20 inches of red streamer still clenched in her backside. I was impressed. It reminded me of the magic trick where the magician pulls the handkerchief out of his hat and the handkerchief is about a mile long. I wondered how much was in there. It also reminded me of the toy cars I had as a kid. They had rip-cords on them and when you pulled the cord, the cars took off like...well...scalded dogs actually. Every time I pulled the table cloth, the dog got faster. I've had rope burn before but never there. I can only imagine the agony. Anyway, I finally got the table cloth out and the dog healed up nicely. I only use that table cloth now when the in-laws come over.

All three of my dogs were stray animals that found permanent residence with me. I have a hard time saying no. Even if I did say no,

I've learned that none of my dogs speak English. I wish they would learn though, because my Greyhound has beautiful penmanship but I never have any idea what she's writing. I think it's Portuguese.

Larry and I have really developed our non-verbal communication skills. There was an unwritten understanding between us when I had to take him in for his ballectomy and it continues to this very day. I had been hesitant about taking in a giant Rottweiler when I had a one year old daughter in the house already. Larry seemed to really like children but I wasn't sure if he was just one of those people who plays with his food or if he was a really good dog. I remember the day that I became certain that his demeanor was safe for children. I remember, because this was the day I granted Larry full citizenship in our household. I felt like he earned it.

My one year old daughter was already so good at walking that she could do it while eating waffles. She was literally impossible to keep seated at the table. I did not permit my daughter and Larry to have unsupervised visits at this stage of their relationship but on this particular morning, I let Larry into the kitchen while my daughter and I had breakfast. Larry kept his distance but his eyes darted back and forth between our waffles like he was watching a tennis match. He was waiting for something to drop so that he could eat too. My daughter seemed to realize that Larry might want to enjoy a savory waffle too. She immediately embarked on a mission of good faith to deliver what was left of her waffle to Larry. I was more than apprehensive and kept a close watch on the situation.

Larry remained motionless as she approached him but the saliva began pouring from his mouth in anticipation. He seemed genuinely perplexed when she did not stop to place the waffle in his mouth. Instead she continued on the other end of Larry and lifted his tail. She seemed to know exactly where the waffle should go and began the process of inserting it into Larry's behind, which caused me to wonder if my daughter was dyslexic. Larry was not sure what to make of this event and he slowly rose to his feet and looked to me for help. He tried to walk away but my daughter was hot on his trail and actually seemed to be steering him from the back with one hand on his tail and the other hand still pushing the waffle into his butt. The two of them made several quick laps around the kitchen as Larry tried to escape the waffle and my daughter appeared to be water skiing behind him. He looked to me several times for help but I was too busy trying to find my camera. After nearly a full minute of trying, my daughter gave up on using Larry's butt as a toaster, and simply dropped the waffle on the floor. Larry promptly ate it and eventually the waffle made its way back to Larry's butt anyway. You can't fight the inevitable. But at least Larry kept what was left of his dignity and that earned him membership into the family. Any dog that can take that kind of abuse is safe for your kids to play with.

Never say goodbye

Advice is a tool that should be used more like a handgun than a hand grenade. It is intended to be delivered to a specific target and not just tossed randomly into a crowd. There is a perfectly good reason why doctors prescribe medications to individuals as opposed to just putting it all in the community water. Advice is simply not a "one size fits all" kind of thing.

If you have two people standing side by side and one person is being turned down for job opportunity and the other person is about to be hung in the town square, you'd have wildly varying results in just shouting out indiscriminately to both of them, "Hey buddy, keep your chin up!"

If you've got a young child taking a dance class and a serial killer holding you hostage in the woods, you might want to reconsider to which of them you carelessly tossing out these old clichés: "Just follow your heart. Be yourself. Listen to your instincts".

Alas, I can beg you until the end of time that if you can't stop your unsolicited and mechanical dispensing of sayings like: "It's going to get worse before it gets better", then you should maybe not apply for a job working the suicide hotline. But you won't listen. Why? Because people just want to talk...all the time...even when they have nothing to say. ESPECIALLY... when they have nothing to say.

The worst phrase ever coined is this one: "Uncomfortable silence". There are more times than not where the most comforting thing you can do for others is to remain completely silent. When two strangers approach each other on a dark street at night, there is some kind of unwritten rule that you are supposed to look at each other, nod, mumble some rhetorical salutation, and possibly even respond. While you might be glad to hear them say anything other than "BOO!", or "This is a robbery!", what you really would like is if, just before you passed this person on the street, they accidentally stepped into an open manhole and disappeared altogether. The only real conversation you ever wanted from them was to maybe hear them scream "Ahhhhhhhhhhhh" as they fall into the darkened abyss of your city sewer system. Then you wouldn't have to ask the obligatory, "How you doin?" while hoping that they don't answer.

It's one thing to pretend to be friendly, but it's another thing altogether to have to actually BE friendly with every stranger you come in contact with. It would take you a week to walk to a public bathroom if you had to shake every hand on the way. Ultimately, what you'd end up with would be a hallway full of people engaged in unwanted conversations while soiling themselves because they never got to the restroom. Personally, I'd rather see you walk by in silence than have you have to explain to me why your poop just fell out of your pant leg and onto your shoe.

Perhaps even worse than starting an unwanted conversation is not knowing when to end one. This awkward situation can, of course, be avoided by NOT starting the unwanted conversation to start with, but as we discussed, that's not likely to happen since people insist on being so randomly generous about sharing their ability to spit words out.

Once again, the blame for the unending conversation harkens back to the fools who use advice as a hand grenade. Somewhere, way back in someone's childhood, they were likely instructed things like, "To have a friend, you must first be one", or "Speak now or forever hold your peace". Sadly, the cure could have come before the disease if someone's grandma had just knitted a pillow saying: "Sometimes it's okay just to shut the hell up". But instead, that pillow said something cuter and incorrect, like: "Your opinion matters".

Thus, we are left with people who start conversations at inappropriate times and then don't know when to end them. Let's just say that you are on the bomb squad and working to diffuse a bomb on a busy downtown street. Ten bucks says that if there weren't other cops there to keep people back, one person would wander up and say "Whatcha doin there pal?". Even though it's MAYBE not the time to talk, they would continue.... "That looks scary. Ever worry that whoever put that bomb together was colorblind? You know, MacGuyver always cut the red wire, but if someone was color blind....you know....BOOM!".

That's an example of a unwanted conversation, and also of one that goes on for too long. Sure, in this case you have the unusual luxury of having a bomb at your disposal so that you CAN just go ahead and cut the wrong wire and put both of the conversation participants forever out of everyone's misery, but typically, you won't be blessed with this sort of option. Sadly, because you don't usually have that bomb, things still have the chance to get worse.... This is the point where the linguistic whore, who is assaulting your personal space has remained completely impervious to your silence and your unanswered prayers for sudden hearing loss, resorts to a conversational tactic that you didn't even know existed until just now...THE IMAGINARY SEGUE WAY. The imaginary segue way is when a person just randomly transitions from one topic to the next without any prodding or logic at all. Typically, this begins by misuing a phrase such as "It's like..."

"You know, MacGuyver always cut the red wire, but if someone was colorblind...you know...BOOM!..... IT"S LIKE when I was a little kid and my mother used to duct tape me to a telephone pole while she worked inside the strip club....

WHAT?!?!?!?! It's not "LIKE THAT" at all!!!!! But it happens...and you can't stop it. Or maybe you can. Start with the children. Knit that pillow that your grandma never did. Spread the word. Sometimes... it's okay to just shut up.

I'll take both

I've put a lot of work into being this fat and sexy. I REALLY like food. It has nothing to do with being hungry. You don't get a body like mine by discriminating against many foods or by skimping. I think I mentioned this already but I'm a fatty. I'm not nearly as ashamed as I should be. I've never been one to suffer under the oppressive thumb of moderation. I eat with a purpose. The Food Network on television is like porn for me.

Let's face it, two things drive a man to get out of bed and hunt each day. Those things are food and sex. And of the two...I can GET food. And the fatter I get, the less I care about sex. I look at it like this....I'm a B cup now too so what can YOU do for me?

Sometimes I feel guilty because my wife has had the common courtesy to remain attractive while I have gorged myself into the world of elastic pants and man boobs. So on fleeting occasions, I've tried to exercise. I love off-road bicycling despite the fact that is indeed exercise. I used to ride quite a bit actually. I recall one of the last great stands that exercise made against the overwhelming army of fat cells in my gut. It was quite a heroic effort, but much like the Alamo, the battle was won by the numbers. Allow me to share the tale…

It was early February in Indiana. The temperature was somewhere shy of zero. I had been bicycle riding in Southern Indiana for many hours and I was exhausted. I made the trip home and was still frozen to the bone and malnourished from the event. I needed food and I craved warmth. I figured that some hot water would do the trick for getting warmed up so I began to draw a hot bath. The 60 year old plumbing in my house worked at a very leisurely pace so I knew I had at least ten minutes before the bath was ready. I went to the kitchen for a quick snack.

The quick snack turned into something more. I made an entire box of macaroni and cheese and a one pound cheeseburger with all of the toppings. It looked outstanding. I was preparing to eat when I remembered the bath. I ran to the bathroom and shut off the tub before it overflowed with warm, inviting water. I was faced with an immediate dilemma. The bath was warm and calling out to me. The cheeseburger was also warm and calling out to me. Something was going to get cold! ….Or was it? I slipped into the bathtub with a nice big plate of macaroni and cheese and giant cheeseburger. I was a single guy in paradise. I got warm. I got full. I got sleepy.

I woke up about an hour later, still in the tub and freezing my wrinkled butt off. Little pieces of macaroni were floating all around me. The burger was gone. The only part of my body besides my head that was sticking out of the water was my enormous belly. And perched upon this island of fat was the plate and it's remnants of a once mighty meal. Each breath raised and lowered the plate to the surface of the water like a ship being tossed about at sea. It was tragic. I knew I had issues. That story haunts me to this day. But it was still a really good meal.

Shipwreck

Someone recently asked me what the worst thing I've ever done was. I don't know what prompted that question but I haven't slept well since I was asked it. I ended up having to make a list and try to narrow it down from those choices. It was a sad commentary on my life. It got even sadder when I ran out of paper. I was honestly disturbed enough that I eventually had to start a second list of the good things I have done in my life. I'm not sure that helped. One list is considerably longer than the other.

It's strange to me. I stop and help people with car trouble about 20 times a year. I always get the door for a lady. I donate money to charity even when I'm too poor to do so. I'm always good to animals and I always try to treat people with respect. I have a good job, a nice house, a great family, and a good education. I thought I was a pretty good person until I made my list. As it turns out, I'm a heathen. Not just an ordinary heathen either, but a really genuine bottom feeding dirt-bag sack of crap.

This little book has been a real eye opener for me. Everyone should write one. It's hard to comprehend what others must think of you until you see your life in print. It doesn't read the same way it does when it's just in your mind. Sometimes when I'm driving down the road, I'll see something that reminds me of a story. I've forgotten a lot of things. It's scary to see them all together. I really feel the need to validate my existence with the story of something good right now.

The problem is that I don't have a story like that.

The list of good things I've done is starting to include things like: I haven't killed anyone yet. I've not yet single handedly caused the downfall of an entire civilization. I have not created or spread any diseases. I rarely leave food on my plate. I have good dental hygiene. I'm good with kids. There is not a picture of me in the Post Office. Nobody can prove anything about that night in Paris with the dead squirrel, two pairs of pliers, and a Congo drum.

I can pinpoint the exact moment in time that my life went from good to bad. I was only thirteen years old when it happened. Accordingly, I can blame all of the bad things I've done since that age on the Harry Chapin song "Dance Band on the Titanic". Thirteen was a wonderful age for me at first. I was in the eighth grade at school. This was my last year as a child in my eyes. I was a full fledged teen-ager. I was the king of the middle school. The girls were starting to change and I was enjoying every moment of each blossoming young woman. I was even starting to grow my own horrible fuzzy attempt at a mustache. Life was grand.

I had a music class that year in school. As you now know, the only music in my body leaves me in the form of a fart. I have no other musical ability at all. I sing in a monotone howl, and I have the rhythm of an epileptic rhinoceros. Ironically, I was getting a perfect grade in my music class because I was smart enough to mouth the words instead of really singing. I even knew all of the correct lyrics to fake. On this particular day I was mouthing the words to Harry

Chapin's "30,000 Pounds of Bananas". My music teacher was a very proper German woman in her sixties who always wore heavy wool turtleneck sweaters and thick wool plaid knee length skirts, regardless of the weather. The music we listened to was all played through her old portable stereo system and her extensive collection of vinyl records.

I was sitting in the front row of the class, between a juvenile delinquent named Jimmy and a big kid named Brian. Brian was singing loudly, I was faking it, and Jimmy wasn't even pretending to sing. He was too cool for that.

After the song was over our teacher knelt down to change the record to one of Harry Chapin's other big hits "Dance Band on the Titanic". The song is about the band that continued to play music as the great ship sank in the ocean, killing nearly everyone on board her. As the music began to play, big Brian tapped me on the shoulder. I turned to see what he wanted. He wasn't singing. He was very pale. He said nothing to me and continued tapping me on the shoulder despite the fact that I was staring right at him. I'm not sure he even knew that I was still in the room. Brian was intently focused on something straight ahead of us in the front of the classroom. Whatever it was even had the attention of Jimmy the Delinquent. It was the first time I'd ever seen him look scared.

I looked ahead of me again and still saw only our beloved teacher, kneeling next to the record player. Finally, I saw what they were seeing. Our teacher apparently thought that her thick wool skirt was enough clothing and opted not to wear underwear beneath it. From our seats, we could see straight up the skirt as she knelt before us. I was seeing something that I had not yet seen at my tender young age. I had fantasized all year long about seeing a woman's most secretive bodily asset, and here it was. It was not at all what I imagined. It was 64 years old, German, gray, hairy, and appeared to have been recently starched. I wasn't sure if I was seeing my first actual gateway to human birth or if she was hiding a den of Porcupines in her skirt. I joined Jimmy and Brian in the horrible trance and could see nothing else in the room. I couldn't swallow, breathe, or even look away.

I tried to dismiss the situation as the sad song of the Titanic played to the rest of the class. The rest of the room was singing as our ship was sinking. I wondered if it was even the record that was playing the old Harry Chapin songs. From what I could see, my teacher appeared to have the old gray haired man in a headlock, firmly between her legs, forcing him to sing live while she played a blank record.

Alas, it was not a man in a headlock, nor was it a den of Porcupines. In the prime of my puberty, I was witnessing the twilight of hers. It was an image I will never forget. I began to fail classes after that. I started drinking hard liquor by age 14. My streak of 8 consecutive years of perfect school attendance came to a screeching halt as I struggled to find motivation to get out of bed each day from that day forward. I don't blame her vagina. I don't even blame my teacher for not keeping it in a better cage. I blame the Dance Band on the Titanic. I've been aboard that shipwreck ever since.

Unarmed

I think every man prides himself in being perceived as a model of boundless courage, a fearless conquistador, and protector of helpless women and children. I am no exception. That being said, if I were to ever wake up to a live snake in my bed, I would scream at such a pitch that only dogs in other countries could actually hear it. While silently screaming, my body would also pucker up to half it's normal size, and my anus would then quickly produce a similarly sized chocolately replica of said snake. There, I said it. I'm afraid of snakes. I'm not entirely sure why, but I sort of credit this phobia to my Grandfather, who instilled me with this infallible nugget of wisdom when I was merely a child: "Never trust anyone who can't hold their liquor". Obviously, snakes don't have hands, and thus can't, at least physically, hold liquor. In my book, that places them right at the top of my list of things I do not trust.

I suspect that part of my fear, as with most fears, is rooted in my ignorance of snakes in general. I don't know much about them. I can't tell, simply by looking, which snakes are dangerous and which are not. At least with a dog, you are happy to see it wagging its tail, but that I've never felt that same calming sensation when a snake wags its tail at me.

The perception of evil dates all the way back to the Bible. The infamous "serpent" in the Garden of Eden, I believe, was some sort of snake. Once again, due to my ignorance of snakes, I don't know which kind of snake it was exactly. Given the fact that there was only one man and one woman in the Garden at the time, and that those same two people are credited with spawning all the future of mankind, my money would ordinarily be wagered on the fact that they were referring to the very dubious "trouser snake", but since Adam did not yet wear trousers, I think they probably just called it a "serpent". Still, it's entirely possible that my phobia is increased by the fact that snakes do resemble large, venomous, free-range male sex organs. The idea of those lurking in my back yard terrifies me. Would I be more comfortable if snakes were shaped more like giant breasts? Sadly, I think so. The simple addition of legs would even go a long way. I'm not scared of lizards.

I have only personally had one experience with snakes, and it was not good. In fact, the last time I saw a snake was also the last time I ever saw my friend Kenny alive. Wait, that sounds like snakes killed Kenny. They didn't...unless a snake gave him Parkinson's Disease. However, just before Kenny died of Parkinson's, I had a bad snake experience in his yard. I still associate those two things.

Kenny knew the end was near and asked me to come over and look at some collector cars that he would be selling due to his illness. He had a barn full of fantastic old Ford Mustangs, all covered in dust. I stood in the dark barn in sheer amazement for several minutes before finally opening the larger door to let the sun cast it's marvelous spotlight on these hidden gems. I backed slowly out of the barn to let the panoramic view of this mechanical goodness soak in.

As I took a few steps backwards into the yard, I heard Kenny's soft spoken voice take on a strange tone of "emergency whisper". I didn't understand what he said at first but he was repeating it like endless recording.... "Don't move. Do not move. Don't move. Do not move". Then he pointed, slowly, and with his typical shaking hands outstretched towards the ground at my feet. It was at this point the I realized that I was actually standing ON a live snake, pushing him down into the soft ground. His head was stretched about four inches out of the instep of my shoe and his head was trying to reach up to my leg, but couldn't due to the full weight of a giant and terrified white guy whom was perched solidly on top of his body. About five feet away, sunning itself in the noon day glow, was a second giant black snake, coiled up and motionless, but with its beady eyes fixed firmly on the strange new snake-stepping threat that was myself. A third, and forewarned of, "response snake" began forming in my colon.

I immediately heeded Kenny's advice not to move, which I attribute more to my panic induced paralysis than his cautionary whispers. Kenny walked back into the barn, grabbed something, and turned to walk towards me. Kenny, in his permanent quivering condition, was now wielding a giant axe. "I'll get him for you", Kenny whispered.

About two seconds prior to Kenny's declaration of help, I honestly didn't think there was any creature on God's Earth that would frighten me more than a snake. I believed that because I had not yet imagined an 82 year-old man with Parkinson's and a giant axe that intended to try to cut off the head of a live snake that was only sticking four inches out of a shoe that still contained my foot. I quickly decided this was definitely worse than snakes. I actually might have been LESS scared if it was the snake who was holding the axe. Kenny was about to amputate my foot. I could see it clearly in my mind's eye.

The only thought going through my head was "Does Kenny not fully appreciate how hard it is going to be for me to run from two live and very angry snakes after he cuts off one of my feet???" This was NOT going to be good.

In one of the best negotiations of my entire life, I was able to convince Kenny to hand me the axe, which should have been infinitely more comforting to me. However, once holding the axe in my hands, I realized that Kenny appeared to have handed me his Parkinson's as well. I was shaking like a dance club in an earthquake. The axe was seeming like an increasingly bad idea.

Here I was, a model of boundless courage, a fearless conquistador, and protector of helpless women and children, standing on top of an unarmed creature 1/20th my size and I was the one with the axe. I was also the only one trembling. The prospect of permanent self induced appendage loss inspired me to turn the axe over and use the flat side to bludgeon my underfoot foe to a horrible death. In one fluid motion I leapt from the snake and rained a certain crushing death blow upon the innocent creature.

The event did not go quite as planned however. The axe made contact with the snake but just enough to push it into the ground and then pick it back up on the backswing. As the axe came swinging back up the sky, it was followed into the air by a giant black snake that was twisting through the air like burnt spaghetti in a food fight. The snake bounced about six feet into the air, putting it right at eye level to the man who thought he had just killed it. It was a moment frozen in time as the world seemed to stop. The only sound on the whole planet was the quiet laughter of Kenny in the distance.

I suspect that the snake had not yet landed before I had run an 1/8th of a mile, retrieved my car keys from the depths of my pants pocket, while running, which I assure you is no easy task, started my car and driven back into my county. I never saw Kenny again. Sometimes though, when I drift off into a gentle slumber in the noon day sun, I can still hear Kenny quietly chuckling....

The vision of Kenny with an axe mostly cured me of my fear of snakes. So thank you Kenny. I never got to say goodbye but I think our last memories of one another were far more substantial than a simple farewell. PS...I still have your axe. It was a danger to you and, as I said, I am just "mostly cured". There is still one pissed off black snake out there somewhere and I can't be too careful.

15936107R10119

Made in the USA
Lexington, KY
27 June 2012